MAKEOVER

Remaking Your Life from the Inside Out.

BELINDA JULIAN

BALBOA.
PRESS

A DIVISION OF HAY HOUSE

Balboa Press books may be ordered through booksellers or by contacting:

Balboa Press
A Division of Hay House
1663 Liberty Drive
Bloomington, IN 47403
www.balboapress.com
1 (877) 407-4847

Print information available on the last page.

ISBN: 978-1-9822-1659-7 (sc)
ISBN: 978-1-9822-1660-3 (hc)
ISBN: 978-1-9822-1665-8 (e)

Library of Congress Control Number: 2018913816

Balboa Press rev. date: 07/17/2019

make•o•ver
ˈmākˌōvər/
noun

1. a complete transformation or remodeling of something,
    especially a person's hairstyle, makeup, or clothes.

    Synonyms: transformation, renovation, overhaul, new look,
    remodeling, refurbishment, reconditioning, improvement.

Do you ever have those times in your life? As Oprah would call them "aha moments," where all of a sudden, all the experiences in your life suddenly make sense, the good, the bad, the ugly and everything in between? You realize everything has always been in perfect order, or *divine timing* as some would say. Each experience, every milestone, every breakdown has been leading you to your next breakthrough, driving you to exactly where you are meant to be. That is exactly what this book is for me.

Contents

Blowout

What seem like bad times are usually our biggest lessons, giving us the transformative power to become our highest selves.

blow•out
ˈblōˌout/
noun

A sudden rupture or malfunction of a part of an apparatus due to pressure.

Sometimes our path is obstructed. Objects are strewn here and there.
We don't know if we are making a conscious decision, let alone the right choice.
But sometimes in the grips of indecisiveness, we stumble upon the road we were destined for.

Belinda Julian

I've always been pretty optimistic, believing that with every hardship there is a silver lining and that something good is just around the corner. But along with that was the belief that the inevitable bad times would come back around, kind of like what goes up must come down. I guess you could say I operated as an optimist with pessimistic undertones. Today I indeed believe the rough times hold our most precious nuggets of wisdom and growth, and that there is *infinite good* without waiting for the proverbial shoe to drop. Life doesn't have to be a constant struggle, sometimes letting go and getting out of your own way can be the hardest and often repeated lesson.

I remember when I first decided to do hair as a career. I contemplated for some time, back and forth, with the decision to go to cosmetology school, thinking maybe I should become a nurse or something to make my parents proud. And to be what at the time I considered to be a better service to others. I viewed hairdressing as shallow and superficial, when it hit me that I had to do what was in my heart, even against my dad telling me, "You won't make very much money" and that I would probably change my mind after a year or so. Now here it is almost sixteen years later, and I can say now without a doubt it is an incredibly rewarding profession, and you know what, it is not all about the hair! I have close relationships with almost all my clients, I celebrate, grieve, and share not just my life's ups and downs, but more importantly theirs. I don't just *dress* their hair but, if I can be so bold to say, their souls and spirits. I like most hairstylists believe I am not only making people feel good on the outside but the inside as well. Of course there are the long hours on throbbing feet, a sore back, and exposure to toxic chemicals which are definitely the downside. There's even the occasional difficult client. But what a joy it can be to have someone sit in my chair, maybe they're rigid or scared, or picky. To be able to open them up to trust not only that I will make them look and feel beautiful, but also to soften some of their distrust of people, or fears about themselves. In this way, I know with certainty, this is not the shallow profession I initially thought it to be. I believe I share the gift with other stylists, of not just knowing the look that will fit someone or the magic potion to give them a new or updated persona, but also an intuitive sense of being emotionally whatever the client needs, whether it be a listening ear, words of advice, or just a safe place to set their burdens aside while in my chair and to leave, not only with a new look, but just maybe, a fresh outlook.

At the end of my hair story I will say more about the creation of this book. It may not seem connected, but you'll see that the passion and drives are the same with this endeavor. It boils down to people and the desire for the human connection that I believe we all seek and crave. It's the act of learning about our differences and most importantly our similarities. What makes us tick, what stirs emotions, our stories, our trials and triumphs. There is a common thread, and we are all so much more alike than we are different, more than I think many of us can even begin to comprehend. Maybe I can say all my years behind the chair have led to the culmination of this book. You see even at a young age I just loved talking and interacting with others. My mom said that as a young child I would only speak to hear myself talk. Or as a teenager, I remember being at a friend's house, and I would end up hanging out with their parents. Even way back then I gravitated toward wisdom or knowledge and human connection, always seeking the tapestry that connects us all.

There has always been a quest for knowledge, a search for truth, and the underlining knowing we all are connected. I suppose in some way whether my thoughts of becoming a nurse or becoming a hairdresser or now writing this book, I've always desired to be of service to others and do what I can to lift them up and in any way, be it big or small, make them feel better. It's my way, to do my part in spreading love, positivity, and compassion in the world. To be honest, that's what I believe we are all here for, to use our gifts and use our experiences to polish and shine them and spread them outward to uplift, guide, nurture, and teach others in any way we feel called to do. When we utilize our gifts to the best of our ability, I guarantee there will be at least one person who can benefit from what we have to offer.

This book is my journey which I hope will resonate with you. Now the tricky part, is believing I am worthy and knowledgeable. And that what I have to offer is of real value to others. It's about my lessons and observations, where I have been, and more importantly, where I am going. It's about how I have spent much of my life creating *makeovers* for others and am finally giving myself the *makeover* I deserve, and so desperately need. It has been a longtime coming and one hell of a journey, but I have embarked on this road of inner transformation, working my way outward. I am humbled to bring you along with me and in doing so, I hope to shed some light and awareness in your lives. Let's "*blow out*" the parts of you that are no longer serving who you truly are.

Cancellation

For reasons, unknown, things change and obstacles arise. While this can be difficult, it's merely a way to redirect you.

can•cel•la•tion

ˌkansəˈlāSH(ə)n/

noun

The action of canceling something that has been arranged or planned.

*Letting
go of
sorrow
and regret
will heal you.*

Belinda Julian

As my dad once told me, "If there is any certainty in life, its change". I couldn't agree more. If you're anything like me, change can be an overwhelming and daunting notion. Even though in hindsight, the challenging times turn out to be the most transformative experiences of our lives. Often the wisdom that accompanies them hold our most valuable lessons. When I first had the idea for this book, I was in the midst of a super introspective period of personal growth. I wanted to learn as much and as fast as I possibly could, as if on a spiritual speedway. I thought then I would come back and put together steps 1,2,3 etc. to help you on your way to your best life. I saw this journey as some endpoint, rather than a way of becoming and ultimately, being.

I have learned it's the process, the evolution, an inner way of being that inevitably changes our external circumstances. This book is by no means a quick fix, do x number of things and your life will transform overnight. It's more like when you slowly but surely practice healthy principles while discarding the old outdated ways. Gradually and quite naturally you will embody a whole inner life that will become apparent in your outer life. Just as consistency in diet or exercise brings lasting results. There is no cheat sheet or magical potion. As with any new endeavor, we must do the work, moment by moment, day by day. Sometimes this means going through the emotions and feelings we have long avoided, buried or ignored. It isn't always pretty and most definitely is not easy, but I promise you, it is well worth it.

As we embark on this journey together, I will share some of my experiences and share how I have struggled, clawed my way through, and risen from some of the very things that should have buried me. And even if our experiences differ, believe me when I say, we human beings, souls, have way more in common than differences. We are all together on this crazy, beautiful, and sometimes mad rollercoaster we call life.

If you're anything like most of humanity, even hearing the word *change* can make you run and hide under a blanket for comfort. Even so, most of us know on an inner level that change almost always is necessary being the catalyst that pushes us towards our souls' highest growth. But forging ahead and *creating change*, forget about it! That can leave us with a whole onslaught of doubts; such as Is it right? Am I making the right decision, Will I fail, what could go wrong? etc.

So, while I've always known change can bring beautiful beginnings, I still always fought it, kicking and screaming, preferring to stay comfortable in the uncomfortable. Sound familiar? Only to feel like someone turned on a lightbulb once the change was processed. But still, I fought.

Look, the comfy zone is ah-mazing and should thoroughly be enjoyed, but the reality is, we all know on some level when it's time to start moving. Sometimes we flat out ignore it. Maybe it starts out as a feeling of complacency, boredom, feeling uninspired or lacking a purpose. Perhaps the urgency is turned up a notch. You may be feeling things such as fatigue, anxiety, or just a general longing for something different or new. Sometimes it can even be reoccurring thoughts such as *is this my life*, "do I want to go on this way"? "Is this person, job, relationship good for me? It's as if life is speaking to you, urging and encouraging you to step out of mediocracy and boldly step into your greatness.

And so, we can choose to flow like the vast stream of life, following these prompts, and step by step rise higher and higher. This is where I wish to reside now, but it hasn't always been that way. The other side of flowing is stagnation. I feel when we receive the nudges, whispers, or even blatant screams, and we choose to ignore them, this is when, BAM! we end up in a crisis zone. Maybe it's a breakup with the love of your life, the same love that in retrospect is not the one for you. Maybe it's getting fired from a job, the same job you don't even like. Hell, maybe it's even a sickness brought on that forces you to slow down and pay attention to the stirrings inside you and to take time to nurture yourself. It's like God, the Universe, whomever or whatever your higher power is saying, "Um excuse me, I've been trying to get your attention, and now I must take drastic measures to get you to "wake up, and set you in a different direction".

Now you know when the disasters hit it's very overwhelming, sad, and downright scary. The beauty and strength come from understanding. First realize that something more significant is at play. Look for the blessings in the experience. You see, every single thing, person, and situation is teaching us something. It's shedding light where we need to do some work, usually areas we wish to avoid. So, when you find yourself in victim mode, with all the Why me? What did I do to deserve this? What am I not understanding or seeing? Try not to dwell there for too long. Instead, roll up your sleeves, dig deep and prepare to do some work. What are the messages the lessons are teaching? Are you repeating experiences, the same ones over and over? Are you going against your truth? Are you living someone else's life or truth, maybe your parents, your lover, or boss? Are you stuck living someone else's dream while deferring, numbing or completely ignoring your own? When you can bring truth and awareness to the situation and see your place in it, this, my friend, is when you can start healing and growing towards your best self. Turning trials into triumphs.

In the next chapter, I'll go into more detail, about some of my *blowouts* and major blessings disguised as disasters. How I haven't always followed my own advice and have had to learn things over and over until I got it. How I learned the ongoing process of cancelling the old and replacing it with the new.

Dyed

Sometimes people, places, and things are only in your life for a limited time to teach you a lesson.

die

dī/

verb

Past tense: died; past participle: died.
synonyms: pass away, pass on, lose one's life, expire.

From a hardened bulb, I watched as she sprouted up from the earth. Pushed past all the soil that was meant to bury her. Nurtured with just enough love and light she surpassed all the others and bloomed into the most beautiful flower.

Belinda Julian

L ike most, my life thus far, has been a complete mixed bag. Some confusion, sorrow, faith, optimism, anger, and understanding all rolled into one weird ball. It is quite a strange place when you are in the midst of upheavals knowing it's all for your betterment. Not to make this just about relationships, but they tend to be the most massive mirrors reflecting back to us and teaching us all we need to discover about ourselves. Whether they are intimate relationships, family, co-workers, bosses, etc. More often than not the these relationships highlight characteristics we recognize in ourselves. Or better yet they bring to the surface all that we keep hidden from ourselves.

At different times in my life, I have fallen into the comparison trap and wondered why some people seem to get to coast through life in ignorant bliss, seemingly unaffected by some the more common challenges. The main thing I seem to be compelled by is the notion that I am supposed to do something big. By big, I mean impactful, not necessarily being famous. Rather, doing something that will be meaningful to others. Do something with this insight and sorrow I have processed; If I can touch even one person, it would be worth it. To be honest, I think this is true not just for me, but for everyone. We all have our heartaches and difficulties that make us who we are. I believe we are supposed to share our beauty, our rawness, our vulnerability with others in any way that makes sense to us. Because in that human connectedness, we realize we share so much more than we know or could ever understand.

A little backstory. It's a bit overwhelming as to where to start. For as long as I can remember I've felt people have let me down. Like most people, life has had lots of experiences filled with complete bliss, but the joy seemed to be short-lived. It was just a little taste of if you are "lucky enough" or "worthy enough", this is the payoff.

So, I guess that's where I will start. There has always been a part of me that on the surface believed I deserved good things, but as my experiences have taught me, there has always been a nagging, underlining belief that I wasn't good enough.

Rewind a little bit, and I'll tell you how that came to be. A short recap of the moments that collectively created my story. The same story I would unconsciously carry with me and repeat many times over. The same story I refuse to let rule my life any longer.

I would say I had a pretty healthy upbringing, with school, family gatherings, camping trips the whole deal. Nothing in particular stands out to me. Then at the tender age of about thirteen or fourteen my world as I knew it would change forever. My parents for whatever reason decide to become truck drivers and head out on the road, leaving my brother and me on our own, at least that is my perception of what happened. So, we went from living in a big house in the country on 10 acres, and pretty much-having everything; boats, quads, cows, chickens, a pretty ideal environment, to my parents selling almost all our belongings and setting off for life on the road. My brother went to live with my grandfather, and I went to stay with a friend, and so chaos commenced. My normal life became a thing of the past. My new life would be one of uncertainty and dysfunction. Inconsistency would be my new normal. Shortly after my parents took off, my brother and I began our separate trajectories only to have them interrupted, a reoccurring theme from this point on. My parents ended up getting kicked off the road as their drinking was escalating. The friend and her family I was staying with were suddenly no longer able to let me continue to stay with them for one reason or another.

So, we all ended up back together in the apartment complex my grandpa was managing, a respite you might think. Sadly, that would not be the case. My grandpa was battling cancer, and maybe life had just gotten to be too much, who knows, but my parent's addiction was reaching a fever pitch! My brother was using my grandfather's morphine patches and selling them, which led to a drug deal gone bad, having someone pull a gun on us when we were upstairs in our apartment, you know just the typical day to day activity. Sigh! As more and more difficult and dysfunctional occurrences came to be, I struggled to figure out where my place in the world was. About a month or so after moving into my grandpa's home he sadly lost his battle with cancer.

The place we called home would be no longer. We then found what I guess you would call a four-plex, two apartments downstairs, two up, at what I believe was a discounted rate. Given that my dad is a handyman, he fixed our apartment up for us. There we were again, a lovely, cozy little family. At this point as a teenager, I mostly kept myself busy with friends, not too involved in home life, but little by little - scratch that! All at once my parent's drug use hit an all-time high *literally and figuratively*. I can't say for sure, but I believe my parents were functioning addicts most of my life, but as addiction goes, the functioning part became less. I went from finding my dad doing lines of meth in our old big house to my dad having me go into my parents' bedroom to witness my mom shooting up, thinking that if she knew I saw her doing it that it would make her stop. Sadly, this would not be the case, and again, unfortunately, these sorts of scenarios would become the norm at home.

In a matter of about a month of living in our new place, my mom would lose about fifty pounds, and along with the weight, her sanity. She would continuously pick at the walls convinced there were cameras there. The paranoia so strong she even pulled a knife on me one night because I wouldn't leave my bedroom door open. Needless to say, things were getting out of hand real fast. One night I was out with a friend we were at the local trolley station. We noticed a group gathered around a man who was having a seizure. We walk over to see what was going on and end up meeting two guys. One would shortly after become my boyfriend, and the other I'll tell you about later. So, I end up dating one of them, my first love, the puppy love.

Meanwhile, things back home are next level crazy. Within a month or so the complex we lived in went from normal to being on the verge of getting condemned. I just knew I had to get out, and quick! At the age of fourteen, I went to live with my boyfriend and his family. From the time, we left our big country house, to living at my grandpa's, then the four-plex and now my boyfriend's house; this would become a theme for the next few years of my life. Lots of makeshift families and changing living circumstances. Not exactly ideal for a teenager who is trying to find herself.

So, I lived with my boyfriend and his family for, I can't even really remember how long, maybe a few months, when I guess it got to a point where his family can no longer afford to keep letting me stay. Not really knowing where to go, I randomly end up going with my dad to the house of a woman he knew. When we get to the house, there is a group of teenagers there, and I think "this seems pretty cool" so I end up staying there for a few months. Helping take care of this woman's two small children and trying to pull my weight since I am at this point too young to get a job. I know what you must be thinking! Why would I leave one situation to find myself in a similar ones? Let's just say there weren't a ton of options and at this point, my parents, I believe are staying in and out of random slum hotels and with random people, and my brother was in rehab for drug use.

That left me flitting from place to place, staying with a multitude of different people until the time would come when I could no longer live with them for whatever reason. Long story short, this carried on through another three or four homes, all the while I wasn't enrolled in school, seeing that I didn't have parents to sign me up. No routine, no structure, no love, at least that's how it felt. There was lots of different dysfunction in each of the homes, which had become a way of life for me. You could say as each new situation would come and go, a little part of my spirit *die-yd*.

"Bang" ed

Sometimes we get a little banged around along our journeys.

bang1
baNG/
verb

Past tense: banged; past participle: Strike or put down something forcefully and noisily, typically in anger or to attract attention.

Beautiful chaos donning a bow.

Belinda Julian

L et's jump forward a few years later when the time had come that I finally would move back in with my family. My mom had gotten off of drugs, my brother came home from rehab; we were back in the game so to speak. Although my dad was still using, and soon, found himself in jail after an altercation with a drug dealer. Around that time, I had a one night stand with one of the guys I met while living with the woman my dad knew. There I was, a month before turning seventeen, pregnant.

I remember my initial reaction naturally being scared and even possibly considering having an abortion. But somewhere inside, I knew my son was meant to be and was sent to me, to put me on a different path. Sure, it could've ended tragically; struggling mom etc. But something in me just knew, sort of how I knew, almost immediately, the moment I conceived. Ok maybe it was paranoia, how I knew I was pregnant long before any test or doctor confirmed it. Or how I knew when I had an ultrasound, before the words left the technicians mouth, that I was having a boy. So yeah, I knew my son, my most precious gift, was sent to me. I was chosen to be his mom to change my course and change my story.

I know most everyone wants to do better than their parents, and their parents before them. Look we all do the best we can given our particular circumstances and level of awareness at the time. My son though, is the most beautiful gift I have ever been given and once I made the choice to keep him. I was excited with the anticipation of his arrival. Then it was just me, my mom, brother, and my little bun in the oven. With my dad behind bars, and the revolving door that was our one bedroom apartment; my mom and her giant heart, giving shelter to the many drifters in our small home in the ghetto.

In many ways, this had come to be one of the favorite times in my life. Maybe because of the closeness I feel my family and I shared at that time. Perhaps it's because I thirsted for my family's love, or any type of love for that matter. Maybe it's because my parents were sober for the first time in what seemed like forever and things seemed to be in sort of a flow. Perhaps some combination of both. In any case, I suppose I finally felt grounded for once. We settled into our little routine, my mom and brother working, and visits with my dad. I started working at a pizza place at night so that I could be with my son all day, my mom and brother provided free child care for me at night while I worked. We eventually moved into a larger apartment, stayed there for a while then my brother, and his fiancé took over that place, and my mom and I got another place of our own where we stayed until my dad got released from jail.

Then my parents got a place of their own, and two of my brother's friends moved in with me. It was a convenient situation until it wasn't. My roommates paid the bills, and I bought food and cleaned for my part of the bargain. Which worked for me seeing that during this time, I had a baby, went to school, and was working very part time, not making very much money. It was perfect, for a while. Until the day my roommates decided to plan a move to without letting me know about it, leaving me with all the bills. Shortly after, a girl I was working with offered for my son and me to live with her. So off we went. Only to be told about a month later we could no longer stay because it was military housing, and word got out that my son and I were living there which was apparently against regulations. So, we moved in with my brother for about a year or so until I was ready to be entirely on my own, and had felt I had outgrown the situation. In retrospect, the times when I lived on my own were the most stable periods of my life. Maybe because I felt I was in control?

I've sort of always bounced back and forth between seeking stability outside of myself, typically in the most unstable of places or people, or the other side of the spectrum, just being entirely free of anyone else. Which is, or was, right? Who knows. But it's all brought me to where I am today. I just got a little *banged* around in the process.

After a year or so on my own; my parents were rebuilding their life and wanted to rent a house and save to buy a home. They convinced me to move in with them, which didn't make a whole lot of sense as I was still paying around the same rent. But I really wanted to be able to help them out, and it was nice to have help with childcare when I worked.

I was super close to my family during this time, probably because I craved all that I had missed out on, and although I was now a parent myself, I still, after all, was technically a child who yearned for a family.

Things went well for quite a while, but slowly, little by little my parents started drinking here and there. It went from casual parties and escalated from there. About a year or so later my parents went down to Mexico for vacation, towards the tail end of it, my friend, my son and I went down there to meet them. When we arrived, they were acting pretty strange, and I thought to myself maybe they were drinking and taking pills, as its reasonably easy to get prescription pills in Mexico. We arrive home a few days later, and my parents were hiding out in their bedrooms and still acting weird. I had a sinking feeling in my gut that they were using again. So, when I randomly ran into my mom in the kitchen and asked her if they were using again, she honestly answered *yes*. Panic rising, my fight or flight response activated, I immediately started looking at places, and I moved out about a week later. Not willing to take any chances as to whether this was a two-week bender or not; I was gone, knowing I couldn't gamble on the possibility of being on that sinking ship.

That there is my condensed version of my early years, my adolescent experiences that undoubtedly shaped me, and as you'll read moving forward echoed into my early adulthood. Now we will transition into what I like to call the relationship era.

Mirrors

People are our mirrors. What is being reflected
back to you?

mir•ror

ˈmirər/

noun

A reflective surface, typically of glass coated with a metal amalgam that reflects a clear image.

Too often we fall for potential overriding the essentials, staying absorbed in the illusions; creating scenarios to best feed our egos, rejecting truths and projecting impressions.

Belinda Julian

In my early 20's I thought all I wanted was to meet my someone, my forever, the person I would always be with. I felt like everyone in my family had found their person early on, and just stayed together. Things I didn't consider were that maybe I would outgrow this person, or that perhaps there would be multiple people who would come along to teach me different lessons, and they were just part of the picture, a page in my story but not the whole book. I also used to believe that if two people have a love for each other that you could work through anything. I still believe love takes time, effort and comprise, and do believe in working through things. However, I think we should not compromise our values, integrity or matters that affect us on a soul level.

I will go into what have been some key relationships in my life, my blessings disguised as lessons and the experiences that turned out to be major blessings! Going way back, even early teenage years there was always a little voice in my head that believed I wasn't worthy of love. Or I guess that it would be hard for someone to love me. Maybe on an individual level, I thought it was "normal" as any time you put yourself out there, leaving yourself open and vulnerable, it's scary and can cause the monkey mind to overreact. I'm assuming a lot of people felt this way at one point or another. But again, as we get into my story it'll be pretty evident that a lot of these feelings and thoughts were deeply rooted.

I think on some level I always had sort of teetered between subconsciously wanting to be loved and accepted by anyone and everyone. To the other side of the spectrum of just keeping entirely to myself and not even allowing love to come in, assuming it would be wrong or I wouldn't be "enough." And again, given my story and my life thus far I had every reason to think it would be wrong, that I would be would rejected or abandoned and the opposite of stable which is what I had so desperately craved for as long as I can remember.

Looking back, I had always gone for unavailable men. In retrospect, I suppose I did it because I already knew what to expect and so it fulfilled my negative beliefs and thought patterns, i.e., him not being there for me. On an even deeper level I suppose, you could insert parent issues, as in I couldn't be enough for them to quit drugs and get their lives together. So being unaware at the time, I would continually invite people into my life, my heart, and my home that were emotionally unavailable on some level or another. *This time* I thought I could *prove* I was enough, that I could change them. Mind you, this was more often than not with people who didn't even deserve to share my space. But I didn't see it like that, so I would try with all my might to get people to stay who I knew wouldn't or shouldn't. I guess I thought if I could do that, the way I couldn't with my parents, I would win or be deemed valuable. So, went the patterns I would make and repeat over and over, not even realizing it. It's funny, I always thought I learned from the mistakes of others so I wouldn't make the same ones, and wouldn't have the same experiences. But we do what we know, and sometimes when you are in it you lose perspective. For example, I got pregnant at sixteen, the same age my mother was when she had my brother. Or my first real heartache, when my sons father wasn't as present as I would have liked. Here was this amazing little person I loved more than anybody has ever loved someone, and I just couldn't comprehend how you wouldn't want to be a constant part of that love and beauty.

Which tapped into my codependent patterns of trying to make, coerce, cry, complain and control the people around me. My son's father was no exception. Trying to get him and others to do what I *thought* they should be doing, such as have a relationship with my son, etc. while trying to do, what in my mind was a favor to my son's father, which was to save him from the guilt I knew would haunt him eventually.

I was always telling him "one day you are going to regret this and wish you were there and you'll never be able to get that time back." I had preconceived notions of how it all would play out. Now I realize it has way more to do with me, than those around me. You see we do what we know, from our level of understanding at the time. Sometimes we inadvertently bring people, places, and things into our reality to prove our thoughts are right! To make ourselves right! I guess you could call it self-fulfilling prophecies.

This is exactly what happened with my son's father. I always thought that, at best he would know his son on some level, and hopefully have some semblance of a relationship with him. But it would be me who would instill morals, teach my son how to be a kind person, basically, raise him with little to no help.

I always assumed people wouldn't show up for me or my son, and then take matters into my own hands because guess what, that feels *safe*! Or more correctly, it was predictable. When he or anyone else doesn't show up, it's like oh well, so and so is unreliable blah, blah, blah. Good thing I wasn't relying on them anyway. In some sick way, I would always pick out those who would disappoint me because then I get to stay the victim, then there are no surprises. Pretty crazy, huh? I'll go into a few more stories delving deeper into the murky waters of all that has been, and maybe you'll find some similarities to your own story. Perhaps you are *mirroring* some of the thoughts or feelings I have expressed.

Bleached

*Letting others strip away your light by staying in
a victim mentality, and giving away your power.*

bleach
blēCH/
verb

Past tense: bleached; past participle: bleached
Whiten by exposure to sunlight or by a chemical process.

I 'll go into some of my more serious relationships, both the magic and the mayhem. I was still acting out and experiencing more of the same, unavailable men. Different situations, different faces but same outcome. Whether it was all the men, who didn't want a commitment, were already involved in other relationship. I never realized that I felt undeserving and like I had to prove I was worthy by going overboard. It was a futile attempt, since most of them were full of broken pieces. I didn't recognize that I sought fragmented people in hopes that they would suture my own broken parts. Apparently, none of that worked, and I had to learn this unfortunate truth over and over until I got it.

I think in some ways growing up in chaos and dysfunction, I learned to be hyper-aware and to intuit the motives of those around me, ultimately to keep myself safe. So, at a young age I tried to control the lives of those around me, to no avail. All the while I was becoming completely numb and disconnected with myself. I could see and feel other people's emotions and share the best advice for whatever circumstance they were in. In the process, I lost touch with how I felt and what I needed. And thus, gradual destruction of all the things I thought my life should, would, and could be. Contrast that to getting crystal clear, intentional and being totally selfish. Taking time, by the way, isn't selfish at all. Time for self turns out to be what I've always needed. Seeking everything I thought eluded me, in the most sacred, unassuming place. Myself.

Up to this point my life there had been two significant relationships, and a few minor crushes, and some random flickers sprinkled in between. All with the same reoccurring theme of being unavailable; whether they were random flings or emotional entanglements. Men who were in relationships with drugs or alcohol or other substances. Men who blatantly did not want or were incapable of a relationship. Pretty much all the types of emotionally unavailable you can think, of I dated. "Hey, I can love you so much that you'll eventually love me back"! It sounds so ridiculous. And it was.

Looking back, it was me not recognizing that this void I felt internally was so intense that I just grew accustomed to looking for love and acceptance in all the wrong places, ultimately resulting in the rejection of myself. I kept bringing others into my orbit to drive that reality home bit by painful bit! Really quick before it gets super depressing, in all of this, there were, the beautiful moments sprinkled in that taught me a lot as well. Thank goodness all of my enlightenment didn't occur strictly through catastrophes! We're heading to the part where I finally got tired of learning the same lessons over and over again. Then I can share some of the beautiful transformations I've experienced. First, we will delve into what I guess you could say was my FIRST adult love/significant romantic relationship/ learning experience.

Now, remember the boys my friend and I met at the trolley station? Well, one I dated when I was fourteen, and the other I hooked up with ten years later. We reconnected online after years of not seeing each other. This is what I call the relationship era, falling in love, out of love, break-ups, break-downs, plenty of breakthroughs and everything in between. I initially thought it would be great to catch up with my long-lost friend. My girlfriends, on the other hand, were already planning our wedding in their heads. So, we met up for dinner and it was instantly an all-encompassing whirlwind romance, from our date over chips and salsa *my favorite* we would become pretty much inseparable. Now, you know how this whole falling in love business goes. This time it was just a few weeks in when he told me he could picture us together forever *insert the church bells and hallelujahs*. I had always craved the stability of a forever love. I was a goner! What's the saying? Hook line and sinker? It was a crazy, obsessive, all-encompassing love. I/we fell hard and fast! I would later come to realize he did this with every single woman he was involved with, but that wasn't the way I was. I was utterly smitten and consumed in our love story.

Now right out the gate one of the blessings was that I knew him before our intimate relationship, so I felt completely safe falling madly and deeply into that crazy stupid innocent kind of love. I don't know if I would have ever experienced that had it not been for him. But the blessings also made the fall that much more painful. It seemed to be a perfect love story. We knew each other's checkered pasts when we were both directionless teens. He was in love with me all those years back. We now both had young children. We were practically an instant family, all I had secretly yearned for all rolled up into one complicated package. We co-parented, built a home and life together, as best we knew how.

In some way major relationships played out significant parts of my past, progressively getting more tragic and eye-opening as they progressed. This relationship while mostly right, still in my mind and probably in his, left something to be desired. We got along pretty well as best friends do, joking and prodding one another along with some of the normal upheavals that blending a family might typically entail. But like they say, you usually date someone like the parent you have the most healing to work through, in my case it was my dad. This relationship was me dating the child-like version of my dad and in addition to the addict that was my father. More about that later.

Though this relationship had its brilliant times, I seemed to desire and need more. Maybe it was him. Perhaps it was me. I have the sneaking suspicion it was a combination of both of us. He was very immature and insecure which brought out the co-dependent in me. He always seemed to care a smidge too little and me a dollop too much. And if I'm honest, I always had a nagging feeling sometimes it was louder than others that he would let me down in some way. My projections, with him mirroring what I believed to be my truth, combined with his issues, turned out to be the perfect storm.

So, what do you suppose happened? Ding, ding, ding! You are correct! Precisely what I projected would happen albeit not entirely in the way I suspected it would. This relationship had my intuition firing off. It whispered to me, is this the life you want to live… is this really what you picture for yourself? When we would fight we fought dirty, very verbally abusive; a trait I picked up growing up that seemed like the normal way of conversing, or resolving disagreements. In the beginning his insecurity appeared cute and in my mind equated to how much he loved me. But later, when he would be jealous or insecure about ridiculous things, something in me knew I was being stifled and that I needed to be able to spread my wings.

Another thing I did that set a ridiculous standard, was that I did everything for him which he got accustomed to. Later I would have rage and resentment towards him for being so comfortable and letting me handle everything, when all I wanted was an equal partner on all levels. But once again I settled for less and over did what I felt was lacking; faithful to the co-dependent/ martyr in me while letting the resentment reach a climax! Not exactly a recipe for a healthy, thriving relationship. I felt unheard; he felt unappreciated; leaving us both feeling worn down and depleted. I thought it was a phase and something a lot of couples go through. Even though this was what my emotions and illogical logic were telling me. To be honest, it was the beginning of the whisper, guiding me and letting me know I deserved more.

Something similar must have been happening to him, because one day about three and a half years into our relationship, he blindsides me and tells me he isn't happy anymore and that he no longer wants to be together. My heart sank into my body all the way through the floor to the gates of hell! Ok, that last part was a tad dramatic. But you know where I'm going with this. Anyone who has been through a break up knows the hole it creates in your being; the one where you know logically in time, you will feel better and heal, but at the time you can literally never imagine that happening. You feel as if you are the only one in history that has ever felt this pain, and while many have gone through heartbreak, you are certain they did not hurt this deeply. It feels as though time stands still and will never move forward. If you can relate to this, you also know then the desperation and denial it brings. This is fighting growth on the deepest level; you just want to go back a few minutes where everything was exactly as it *should* be. Back to where it is comfortable. Man did I fight this, for two years to be exact. I felt not only had I lost my lover and best friend, but his family too. I felt like I had lost my identity which at the time was being caretaker to our kids and him.

I had invested so much into him and our family trying to create a life unlike what we had growing up. Trying to provide for our kids what we all never had. Moving forward trying desperately to put back the pieces of my shattered ego. All I could zero in on was the fact that I wanted everything to go back to normal in a very who moved my cheese kind of way. I desperately clung to the idea that in my gut I knew he would regret it! Again, my ego kept me stuck. I saw him through three additional relationships and break-ups, different girls, same dramas. And every time things were rocky, guess who was just waiting in wings for a chance to prove she was worthy, and enough. This girl here! Literally, everyone knew he was a fool. I was just waiting for him to catch wind so we could go back to the *comfortable* the *known*. The same *known* my gut knew longed for more. In hindsight, I would recognize this betrayal for what it was. Which was a betrayal of myself! And yes, on a certain level I was mourning the loss, of him, our family and what I worked for; but on a deeper level what I was really mourning was the loss of myself. Each time he betrayed me and I took him back I was digging myself deeper and deeper. Until going back for what would be the last time, the time I finally listened to my inner self, instead of letting my shattered ego feed me ridiculous lies. I finally let go of all my preconceived notions, and stopped searching for my happiness outside of myself, which was where I had lost it! Almost simultaneously I *bleached* a clean space in my life for what would become love number two.

Over Processed

*Getting burned out! Giving when we don't have
it to give.*

To process to too great a degree. This over processed food
barely tastes of anything.

I've always been here for you maybe you couldn't tell,
maybe you were too busy saving the world, Taking on
the next project
Or helping the next wounded person who came along
as they surely always come along.
They are always around, People like that. Drawn to
your light
And the beautiful way you see the world.
They want that for themselves,
Just don't forget
While you were out busying yourself
I have been waiting for the day you returned to the
light
To yourself.

Belinda Julian

I had finally closed a chapter after dragging my feet while simultaneously sticking my head in the sand. Having let the past linger way past its expiration date, thousands of tears, pain, and self-imposed rejection and denial, I finally felt willing to embrace the strange possibility of opening my heart to love again, something I never thought possible. And what do you know, just a few months later that *strange* feeling became my reality! Enter love number two.

We met through a friend who happened to be staying with me at the time. I don't know about you, but it seems after a relationship ending that literally took everything out of me I found someone completely *seemingly* different than lovers of the past. So, where I had always gone for the unavailable, man-children, loud-boisterous, life of the party type of guy, this one was sort of awkward, mellow and very unassuming. To say I was intrigued would be an understatement. Oh and he was crazy handsome. I decided that I wanted to get to know him much better. My friend and I ended up hosting a Halloween party at my house, and I knew with certainty I wanted him to come and to connect. He did, and we did. Shortly after we started seeing each other. The first time after the party he came over to make me dinner *did I mention he was a chef?* It's safe to say I was excited about the possibilities at that point especially after our deeply engaging conversations that night and the days that followed.

I had never really met a man who was so deep, and compelling all at the same time. Even in the early phase, there was a profound soul connection between the two of us. Things progressed for a month or so, just enjoying each other's company. Personally, I was enjoying the respite from heartache, and reveling in feeling excited and alive again. But a few months into the relationship there were some things I started to notice. Like how if we had a few drinks and I would fall asleep super early, he would stay up late being that he worked really late *also, I have narcolepsy – kidding! I don't. I just fall asleep crazy early.* Anyhow, I would notice if I had a large bottle of alcohol and we had had a drink in the morning a significant amount would be gone. Or how sometimes if we only had a drink or two he would seem really drunk *I would later realize he had been drinking before, during and after.* The first time I saw him really drunk, I recognized how he behaved a lot like other addicts I'd known when they are using whatever their *poison* of choice is.

First, I believe they are trying desperately to cover pain and suffering. Well, I saw it in his eyes, just as I had seen in my parent's eyes, pain, darkness, and plain emptiness. It is like the lights are on but no one is home, or they are hiding behind the curtain. I saw the same thing in his eyes, and it scared the crap out of me. This would only be scratching the surface as far as the drinking was concerned. It had my intuition firing off like the Fourth of July. But just as my intuition was begging to be heard so was the codependent, martyr, fixer in me.

There would be some incredible times in the months ahead, mixed with the dysfunction of my dualistic side as I struggled in turmoil over the reality I was facing. On the one hand he was handsome, caring, affectionate, literally thought I was the best thing since sliced bread. In his eyes, I was a Victoria's Secret model. Whereas previous men never really appreciated me, he saw and acknowledged in me all I ever wanted anyone to see and more. It was as if we both could see the perfection in each other the way we couldn't see it in ourselves. To say it was hard to walk away is the understatement of the year. It was damn near impossible and really nothing short of a miracle. Ultimately, I consider it divine intervention. As things steadily unraveled over the next year or so, each incident was a blatant sign for me to let go. Again, maybe it had a lot more to do with me than I imagined because as each devastation would unfold, I would hang on just a little tighter thinking I could heal someone else's pain. But in all actuality, I was only postponing the inevitable work that would allow me to heal my pain before anyone else's. And the irony is that in letting go I would genuinely enable healing to take place in both of us.

But it would be a while before this happened. Since I grew up with addicts, you would think things would have been so apparent to me. But when you are in it, you get sucked into a sort of ego-centric vortex and lose perspective. Like when he had lost his grandma and simultaneously told me of some of his hardships, and would wake up shaking so hard that he couldn't even to hold a pen to write. I held onto compassion and understanding, instead of listening to the warning signs, or red flags. I wrote it off as a phase, not comprehending he was a FULL-BLOWN alcoholic. He would undermine things and make it seem like the dui's, job loss, physical symptoms were new developments. Maybe he thought they were but I all to eagerly played along taking his words at face value, ignoring the signs that were screaming at me. Instead, I tried to understand and wanted to be there for him, wanting to see this addict through in the way, I hadn't done with my parents.

After countless catastrophes getting so out of hand, he went to stay with family for six months, to get help. I should have let go then, but I didn't. Or after the six months was up following a strict treatment. I was moving into a new home, and I knew in my gut it wasn't a good idea for him to move in, but he seemed so excited! And when he suggested he move in, against my better judgment I said yes. Things were amazing with a capital "A" for a small-time period, but chaos returned. Of course, it did. That was my pattern. It goes great, I expect another shoe to drop, the shoe drops, and I'm perplexed. Boy did the shoe drop! Over and over again. Everything from finding hidden bottles, him sleeping all day, going on week benders, trips to the hospital to detox. kicking him out, him staying in hotels, crashing cars, being brought home from work drunk, visits from the cops.

And through it all was the whispering voice in my soul, *get out, get out*; like the slow constant drip of a leaky faucet. Get out, get out! Your life is meant for so much more! I kept putting off the inevitable. Because. Well because of a lot of things; we loved each other, I didn't want to be alone. Fear of starting over, and a whole onslaught of errant thoughts that had nothing to do with logic. Ultimately, I was ignoring the whisper, ignoring the nudges. Until disaster hit one right after the other, making it entirely impossible to lie to myself any longer. The rejection of truth was no longer an option. I came home the day after Thanksgiving after working a super long day, to find him drunk *again* deciding I was in no mood to deal with it. Shortly after, I hear a loud bang on the door. It was the police! I guess he had been on the phone with his brother and was so drunk his brother got worried and called the cops. The cops then seeing him in his obliterated state thought it best to take him to the hospital to detox. Meanwhile the next day we were set to go to my grandma's about five hours away. Needless to say, I left without him.

When I returned home the next day, assuming he'd still be in the hospital, I see what clearly appears to be pieces of his car spread across my driveway down the path! Horrified, I saw that it got worse as I turn further down to see my fence completely wiped out! Once I made it inside the house it looked much the same, things were haphazardly splayed all over, everything broken all around. It looked like it had been hit by a tornado! He was nowhere to be found, and I immediately call the cops. While they were on the way, I located the suspect I called my boyfriend, with the police arriving shortly after. They tell me they can't make him leave although I desperately needed him gone. Funny by the time I was really done, I technically had no rights to make him leave.

Seeing the frustration in my eyes, one of the officers offered to bring a mental health specialist over. After she spoke with him and recognized he was obviously seriously depressed *you have to be to drink that much*. I'm assuming he admitted being suicidal and they took him away on a Fifty-One fifty; Being a danger to yourself or others. Only for him to show up the next morning already drunk again.

So, for almost the whole duration of our relationship he would get caught drinking, and he would do better for a while and be utterly amazing, start slipping, then go on a two to seven-day bender, get out of control, get scared, go to the hospital to detox, round and round. Again, I can't say why I stayed so long. Co-dependency, wanting to save a broken person and see him through. As long as I focused on helping others I prolonged and postponed healing the broken, rejected, abandoned little girl in me. The one that wanted desperately to be enough to make the unavailable addict see that if they chose her how great life could be, and how happy she could make them.

But what I was really doing is putting off doing that for myself. So, there I was, sending this man I loved off on a greyhound to be with family in Fresno, a place he had long avoided and dreaded. After having the sobering reality brought on fast and furiously, from the whispers, to nudges, to shoves, I had tried so hard to avoid, I knew I had to let go, stop feeding my ego that thought I was just loving and helpful. I had to realize we both were no longer growing. He needed to be truly uncomfortable and accountable for himself if there was any remote chance he would be able to come out of fighting his demons alive. Well, I had my own monsters to face; truths to unravel and beauty to uncover. And I wasn't going to get there clinging to the past, that was for sure. To say I was *Over processed* would be a complete understatement.

Reschedule

After a change, sometimes we need to regroup, reroute, and redirect.

re•sched•ule
ˌrēˈskejəl/
verb

Change the time of (a planned event).

One day it'll all make perfect sense
the no you wished was a yes
the turbulence and upheavals
the heartbreaks that catapulted you into a cocoon
to emerge a captivating butterfly
so, until then stay strong
fake it till you make it if you must
and know one day it will all make perfect sense.

Belinda Julian

Speaking of clinging to the past, boy oh boy was that ever a crutch of mine! Even in the midst of these upheavals and the grand finale. I knew it wasn't right, but I thought I could just keep holding on a little longer as if grasping tighter would make it less painful. WRONG! Every time I would find a bottle, my intuition would yell GET OUT, this isn't the life for you! Every time we would be having a great day running errands or spending time together, I would think, "this is wonderful", and I would smell a whiff of alcohol, and I would start to panic. Even waking up to the voice in my head shouting GET OUT, *divine intervention* wasn't enough. I would lie to myself a little more, "maybe I'm crazy, maybe I'm imagining things or being paranoid, maybe I have it all wrong". His addiction, was bringing to the surface all the things I needed to heal within myself. There I was, practically having my past regurgitated in my face, and I had nowhere to look but inward. What am I learning here? Why does dysfunction surround me? Why do the same situations keep showing up over and over, different faces, but same storyline? I had to really sit with myself and ask some hard questions and think about what the common denominator was. And the answer was me. What part was I playing in this mess of a life I was living? I could feel it bubbling beneath the surface. Something was telling me that I was destined for a more significant life than this. Hell, we all are, we just have to shed all that life has piled on us that isn't who we really are. Maybe we don't even realize a better life exists or is possible. But sometimes in the midst of the madness, we get a little glimmer or recognition within ourselves, that life doesn't have to be a constant struggle and sometimes that little glimmer can be the start of brilliant illumination. But it wouldn't be quite that easy for me nor quite that fast. I had a lot of undoing and uncovering to do. I guess you can say that is what the majority of this book is about; tons of unlearning and undoing within myself. Not just the crazy stories we, or others, tell ourselves and believe to be true. Moreover, the things we let our ego determine to be true. For example, I found myself in situation after situation thinking I was a victim of circumstance, that others were incapable of loving or being there for me and so on. That was what I believed, so of course it showed up time and time again! I didn't know or expect anything different. But that voice is the first sign, a seed planted. It was my higher self, god, the universe or whatever you want to call it, guiding me; guiding me back to real perfection; who I was before I let situations outside of myself determine who and what I was. What I could achieve, experience and receive. I'd like to think I have always been a seeker of sorts; seeking the truth, and on some level believing in something bigger than myself, and that everything always happens for a reason. But it was a very vague and flimsy belief. What my experiences, have taught me is this;

There is most certainly a force much greater than we could ever comprehend, guiding and teaching us, through life circumstances and the people in our lives. You can call this force god, source, the divine, spirit. I think this divine source meets you where you are and however you can best be reached. So, whether that is a god, Buddha, the universe, angels, guides, spirit or all of the above, it does not matter. It's whatever resonates with you. Let's just say there is an unseen team, gently, subtly guiding us to our highest, best version of ourselves. And they know with a clear, unobstructed overview the real perfection that we are. They have a clear vision of what our lives are supposed to look like. They will deliver the exact person, place or thing in whatever way is appropriate at that moment, time or phase of our life that will help us evolve into the truest, most authentic versions of ourselves. That to me is what everything happens for a reason means. Each experience, the good, the bad, and everything in between is teaching us! Continually waking us up more and more. Waking us up to all that is not flowing in our lives, all that is broken in need of repair, all the dark spots hidden in our psyche in dire need of light. And at any given moment in our lives, we are receiving the lessons and the growth, and discarding all that doesn't serve us anymore. I would say this is the true spiritual journey and though everyone's is quite different, I believe we are all doing this on a regular basis whether we realize it or not.

This time in my life had been a HUGE eye opener and the start of a spiritual awakening for me. It began with me being a humble gatherer, collecting knowledge in whatever form I could. Desperately seeking answers with an urgency to feel what most of us long to feel; safe, in control, and a sense of connection. And the road leading to all of those things is a lot closer to home then we realize. The journey of a thousand miles or lifetimes truly begins and ends in the same place. Within. What this meant for me personally was owning for the first time how I was the people pleaser. I had to get solid in myself and quiet enough to hear my soul's callings. What is needed, what it wanted, and had been deprived of while I was so focused on everyone around me all those years. After really getting clear within myself I recognized I do love to help others, but I had just been going about it in a counterproductive way. There will always be that side of me sees other people's sufferings and wants to take that away. But I had to learn to use those gifts in a way which was not harmful or draining to myself.

Learning to use them in a way that serves my higher calling and is coming from a place of abundance, not from a fearful, ego based place of trying to fill a void within myself that wasn't serving anyone. But again, nothing is ever wasted as EVERY

circumstance is working out for the best whether we can acknowledge that or not. With that, this time in my life had a strange air about it. You know that weird feeling when things are falling apart but you know deep within they are coming together? When you feel like you have so much wisdom and knowledge, yet you don't know anything? You are only scratching the surface. When you try as best as you can to make sense of all the whys, and try to figure out the lessons in the midst of the madness. While I think I have become the attentive life student, it turns out I had to learn some lessons over and over before I got it! What's the saying what we resist persists? Meaning whatever we don't learn will show up again and again wrapped in a different package, but the message will be the same. So, in the midst of this uncertain period, having had an alcoholic boyfriend, amplifying my past so that it begged to be healed. Here are some observations: Listen to my intuition. Let go when things aren't working, or more importantly when they're going against my truth. And the BIGGEST one, you cannot change people or be enough for them. Being *enough* was a big running theme in my life. Worry about having *enough*, being *enough*, but *enough* for what, and for whom? Ultimately, it's all there inside us. It has taken a lot of hard lessons to get to a place where I could start dissolving those self-limiting beliefs. Beliefs I undoubtedly picked up early in life. Having addict parents, you want to be able to get them to stop using and it can become an endless pit of hope based fears. Hoping it will be different, hoping they will change, that you will be good enough for them to want to. All the while having this urge to stay, to have things change, the extreme fight or flight reaction to get out before it gets really bad and you get sucked in. This had been my life in a nutshell. As much as I had thought I had grown and evolved, there was still the little girl inside that didn't want to be alone and desperately wanted someone, anyone she could count on. I had gotten into the habit of being there for everyone, when I really just wanted someone to be there for me, and for once in my life not to be let down, to be there when I need support. To be heard. To be loved. This is the condensed version of what had become my story. Story meaning what I carried with me throughout my life, what I embodied, and what ultimately followed me around like a dark cloud casting a shadow on everything I encountered. This feeling of unworthiness, fear, trepidation, and lack of trust, more than a distrust of others was the distrust of myself. It had taken these recreations of my past both, the small and large, to finally raise my awareness to contemplate how I had been living my life thus far. What circumstances was I settling for, what truths I was avoiding and denying. Undeniably leaving me cracked open to make peace with my past, have contentment within myself and my present so I could boldly step into the life I was meant to live. The life that we are all meant to live. By *it* I mean rescheduling who and what we allow in our lives.

Cut

Making conscious choices to cut out unnecessary drama and negativity in our lives.

cut
kət/
verb

Make an opening, incision, or wound in (something) with a sharp-edged tool or object.

*Through the stormy weather of whichever season of our
life, we find ourselves in
Just know rain cleanses and clears away
Clouds disperse and float away
And the sun always shines again.*

Belinda Julian

Cutting out negativity from our lives.
Maybe that sounds scary, or has you feeling overwhelmed as to where to even start. As with hair sometimes it's a little too nerve-racking to make the big cut. So maybe let's start with small snips, trimming regularly. Some hairstylist may have told you that "trimming your hair" helps it grow. And you may have wondered how the heck is that possible when the hair grows from your scalp? How can the ends make a difference? Although you can let hair grow for long periods of time without trims, thinking the dead ends have no effect on the rest of the hair. Though initially it won't, eventually the dried out, broken or split ends will start gravitating up the rest of the hair shaft creating havoc on your hair. The same can be said for negativity in our lives, be it people, behaviors, or thoughts. Although it can be hard to make the big cut, without intervals of regular trimming the broken ends of our life can work their way all the way up to the root of our being, weighing us down, and tangling us up. This is when life will step in making the big cut for us. The same one we tried so desperately to avoid, much like the dry tattered ends, we hold onto for various reasons, comfort, familiarity, or just plain unwillingness to change.

The same can be said of the negativity the surrounds us in our daily lives. We will start with people, we all have them in our lives, the energy vampires I like to call them. After being in their presence for any extended period, we find ourselves walking away feeling drained, frustrated even emotionally depleted. They can show up numerous ways, from the person that just talks and talks, making everything all about them, never once taking as much as a second to inquire about you and your well-being. Maybe it's someone who is verbally abusive, or that puts you down to make themselves feel better. Or the chronic gossiper, religiously talking bad about others and trying to drag you into it with them. Last but not least are the constant complainers, always griping about the latest drama to plague their lives. We may even have a bit of those character traits in us ourselves. Aside from cutting these types of behaviors or people out of our lives completely, if that doesn't seem quite possible to you, is a definite call for boundaries. What, moving forward, are you willing or not, to accept or keep in your life? *This is part of the makeover process.* Boundaries, especially with those whom we are close to; particularly family members can take some time, and often require separation to implement. When people are used to you accepting or putting up with certain behaviors they will be hell-bent on keeping you in that same place. First is getting clear within yourself what kind of energy and people do you want to be surrounded by; Then notice how certain situations make you feel. Do they build you up, leave you feeling lighter and brighter? Or do you feel depleted and drained? Feel your way through and then take steps towards the life you want to create. Looking at your behaviors, and thoughts is the priority. After all, we only have control over ourselves. Maybe you are the chronic gossiper, complainer, or negative Nancy. Looking back, I recognize I have been all of these at different points in my life, sometimes all simultaneously. For example, I have certainly engaged in my fair share of gossiping. Interestingly, my young adolescent self-knew more about this than the adult me.

I remember being in middle school, and chatting with a friend, in what I recall being my first bitch fest. She was complaining about a girl, who was beautiful and charming, and quite honestly had it going on, yet she put her down and belittled her in an ill attempt to make herself feel better. At first, I disagreed with her, only to find myself after a few minutes chiming in adding to the drama. Almost immediately I thought, why do I agree with her, this isn't even true. And I remember feeling super crappy. But it's like I couldn't help myself. I was lured by the feelings of belonging and fitting in. Fast forward to my adult self; I started realizing what younger me knew but didn't act on; that gossip or highlighting the things we don't like in others says more about us than it says about the person we are speaking about. There is the saying whatever we dislike about others is what we dislike or even hate about ourselves. Maybe this sounds crazy to you, but I swear, try it on for size, next time you are griping or complaining about someone else. Sit with it for a few and see yourself in them. Maybe its Tina at work and you just hate the way she always tries to dominate conversations, and you view her as self-centered and annoying. Or maybe you get super annoyed at your father-in-law for being inconsiderate and selfish. Guess who might carry some of those same characteristics? You got it. But here is the really cool thing. Once you start noticing all these mirrors around you it is the perfect opportunity to delve deeper into your reflection and *cut* out those parts of you that are holding you back and keeping you in a negative space.

Next, the chronic complainers *shhh* I used to be one of those. It would be anywhere from *it's hot, these aches*, to bitching and moaning *gossiping* about others around me. Now we all know the chronic complainers, but what happens when perhaps that person is you? First become aware, by that I mean ultra-aware. If it's coming out of your mouth you can bet your ass it is swirling around on repeat between your ears. You may or may not have heard this concept before, if you have, great, it will be a refresher, and if you haven't, it will be some fresh insight. It's that our thoughts create our reality. What we think, and more importantly feel on an internal level, will be reflected in our lives. What does your life look like, what areas are nagging at you, irritating you or making you feel uncomfortable? We all at this point know what my inner dialogue was telling me because it was evident in everything that showed up in my life. Right about now you might be panicking, not knowing where to start. Well if you are the gossiper, make a pact with yourself to cut back *or go cold turkey* if that's your style. Rather than speaking the thoughts into existence, observe the feelings that come up when you think of speaking ill of others and pay attention to the things you need to resolve within. If complaining is your flaw, start observing the words you speak and how it resonates in your body. Are these complaints valid or necessary? Are they just opportunities you use to feel heard, or more likely, keep you stuck, and committed to your victim story, i.e., not good enough, pretty enough, so on and so on. Only you can honestly know the tape that plays on a loop as the soundtrack of your life. But know this, most of us have a relatively similar album playing. Some of us even have the extended version. And know this, you aren't alone. You can take back your life one thought, one word, one feeling at a time.

Thoughts:

Our thoughts create our reality. Anyone who has ever read The Secret, or any other books on the law of attraction, knows this to be true. I remember the first time I read The Secret it blew my mind and if I'm honest scared the crap out of me! There are a lot of dark chambers in one's mind; and honestly, it was so crowded *my mind* like a restaurant at maximum capacity. It overwhelmed me! Think positive, ok crap, now I just thought something negative. Then I get nervous, and keep repeating like a hamster spinning on a wheel going for the most cardio within an hour. But here's the thing. While this concept is, in fact real, whether we believe it or not. Think positive, and it will change your life! For some I suppose this might be effortless, then again, I'm just going to go out on a limb here and assume if we are reading these types of books we are typically searching for the feelings positivity brings. But what if there is so much congestion keeping you from riding the high train of unicorns and butterflies, this is where the undoing comes in. *More of that later.* If you have ever tried to monitor all of your thoughts, you know it's a zoo in there and nearly impossible to wrangle all of the monkeys. That being said, an excellent place to start is your feelings.

Feelings:

How do you feel? Good? Bad? Indifferent? Paying attention to our feelings is the quickest most efficient way to gauge what kind of havoc those monkeys are creating. Also, side note, it is wise to not only observe what is going on, but most importantly to feel it as well. You cannot just slap a rainbow on top of a pile of manure, and expect that once the rainbow vanishes that the manure will not still be there stinking away. Same with our feelings, we can't just throw a positive thought on top of a crappy belief and expect it to dissipate. Well, we can try, but sooner or later it will be right there, waiting to be felt, trying to get our attention with all sorts of adverse scenarios in our head. So, while it sounds nice and simple, happy thought equals happy life, many of us need to plow the shit first! Insert this quote.

It's ok to lose your shit sometimes, because if you keep your shit, you'll end up full of shit.

Then you'll explode, and there'll be shit everywhere.

It'll be a shit storm, and nobody wants that. *~unknown~*

So, let's start tending to our feelings, shall we? After all, the common goal is to FEEL GOOD! Right? Ok then.

Words:

Now we will take a look at the words we speak both to ourselves and about ourselves as well as the words that make it out of our mouth. It might seem of non-importance, but many of the words we use and our affiliation with them trigger feelings in us, which correlates with, you guessed it, our thoughts. Just a great wholly triad these three things! Now obviously I cannot go over the entire dictionary, but we will work on some common words or groupings of words and how they can influence our lives. For example, we might be or at least know someone who is always rushing from place to place, all the while complaining they NEVER have enough time. They think it, feel it, and affirm it that they don't have enough time; So, guess what, it is their reality. Do you think this person can strictly think I have more time, and then poof it appears? Perhaps. Although in this instance I would assume there is a story blasting in the background, of needing to be busy to be important, or not lazy, etc. So, the first step would be the acknowledgment of wanting more time. How more time would make you feel. Feeling the feelings that have you in such a tizzy in the first place, and going through them. Maybe someone, at some point in your life, said or made you feel the only way to accomplish or succeed is to work hard without giving yourself breaks. Maybe the act of staying overbooked is done strategically to avoid feeling anything at all. Maybe you or someone you know, labels things as GOOD or BAD constantly judging themselves. The feelings associated with this are guilt and shame, and false reward. You get the idea now of the narrative we create when we think and speak. Take a few minutes, write down some words or phrases you use on a regular basis. Then write down how they make you feel. Now replace it with a new more positive word or phrase. You might even choose to do away with it altogether. Work with these concepts for a while and revisit them when necessary. Take your time; some might have more work than others, it will all depend on how much you need to *CUT* out.

Root-lift

Revisit the past; make peace with your past, so it doesn't F@#k up your future.

root
ro͞ot/

Raise to a higher position or level.

Like weeds spread out before me growing bigger every day. So are these thoughts and way of being that have taken root in my mind for far too long, left to grow and fester way past their prime. Ignored another day until their presence can no longer be denied, for they have taken over and bombarded all the beautiful thoughts and at last must be tended.

Belinda Julian

On the subject of cutting out; In the same way, an addict will inevitably hit some situation, or a multitude of them, leading them to rock bottom. Finding themselves at a crossroads or fork in the road, where carrying on with the same habits and behaviors will no longer work, and therefore being forced to cut out certain behaviors. We non-addicts can find ourselves in a similar space, where fateful circumstances or beautiful disasters hit beautiful because they are necessary to guide us to change and blaze a new trail. One must also cut away at old thoughts and the negative ties that keep us prisoners to our past; past-conditioning we cannot move forward carrying the disharmony of our past. It starts with forgiveness. You may have heard the tremendous amount of freedom forgiveness will bring but have yet to apply the principles. You may have also heard something along the lines of forgiving someone, doesn't mean you agree with what they have done, or that you think it is ok but rather relinquishes the power it has on you and your life. Believe me, coming from personal experience, I know all too well the effects of holding on too tightly to judgment and non-forgiveness and the torment it created within my body, mind, and spirit, not to mention my life. Although for a while I viewed it as crap, at the time I was committed to staying a victim. And when it's left to rot too long, it can show up as illness or dis-ease in the body. So, perhaps on a certain level you believe this to be true, but don't know how to move forward with this knowledge and turn it into something tangible in your life, leaving you with the lasting relief and the healing it will bring. I used to think I could just simply decide in my mind I forgave someone and all would be well. For a very long time I think I operated from this space as if somehow just saying the words made it true for me; This form of forgiveness might work for some of you. As for me, it had tucked itself away in the crevasses of my being, leaving me feeling a VICTIM! A victim of circumstances, of other people, of life. Just passively surrendering my power, hell, practically giving it away. In other words, rendering myself POWERLESS! Leaving myself void of my power and then blaming it on others. Because we all know it's a whole lot easier to sit around blaming others rather than take a look in the mirror. Maybe we can begin with viewing forgiveness as a vehicle to deliver us to reside in our power. Deliver us peace of mind, and bring us to a place comfort. Personally, this all started and became a new way of being for me when I was able to view the ever-present duality of life, and the spiritual journey we are all on. It has been said that before we incarnated into this life, we choose the life we would be living, knowing in advance the hardships and growth we would experience, and that, in particular, we choose our parents. This concept may be a load of crap, and just a way to help soften the blows that life gave us. But nonetheless it's something I believe. *It does not matter if you believe this.* But it is something to consider, especially if you believe everything happens for a reason and feel the truth of the connectedness of everything. As I've said, forgiveness of some of our early experiences could be especially hard, many have suffered through lifetimes of hurt and pain more than anyone should have to go through. But what if we could look at these circumstances in a new *different* light. Instead of making the primary focus the unfairness of it all, pay attention to the gifts your life has instilled in you. For example, my experiences gifted me with, strong intuition, unwavering ability to empathize and understand others and connect with them on a deep soulful level. So, starting from this awareness I was able to not only fully forgive my parents and my past, but actually, be GRATEFUL for the experiences that shaped me into who I am. Then with some of the compassion and understanding, I have been able to understand that everyone, my parents included, were doing the best they knew how given their level of experience and understanding at the time. To even take it a level deeper, if you are in the space emotionally to do so, even inquiring of whomever is the subject for your forgiveness, about their life experiences, you may notice that.

1. They were repeating patterns and behaviors they learned and experienced. 2. That they were doing the best they could given the circumstances, they came from but most likely never healed from; see how just viewing things in a different light *the light of understanding* can change how you perceive things. Again, none of this is to discredit or diminish your pain or suffering but rather to release the control it has on your life, because ultimately you do need to feel and heal the pain associated with forgiving people, places or things. I have an analogy of sorts, to send the message home a little further. And you may even see pieces of yourself in it. For me an example would be me forgiving my parents. When I was able to hold compassion for them and inquired more about their lives and experiences, I was able to see and feel *forgive* the scared anxious child in them. And realize we aren't all that different, and hopefully they could forgive me for the times I acted holier than thou, thinking I would NEVER be or do things like them. But as I know all too well, life has a funny way of humbling you, and histories repeat even when we think we got away from the patterns scot free. Whether it's new parents bringing a child into the world, or starting a new job, or relationship; generally, everybody starts with the best of intentions, right? But life happens, things get messy and complicated, or just plain hard. Most new lovers, parents or employees don't start off thinking *you know what, I'm going to be really shitty at this.* Everyone has their baggage and

old wounds that they carry around inside of them. Mixed up together, it's no wonder we are all running around in less than desirable states. This my friend is where compassion can double as a miracle, because ultimately it comes down to choices, and the big question is how do you want to FEEL? My guess is you want to feel good, so what do you say, give it a whirl. You deserve it! Once you are at peace and residing in forgiveness of others, the true healing happens *something I almost bypassed, but life took me right back*. This is such a vital piece of the puzzle. FORGIVENESS OF SELF! This process will look different for each individual, but the most imperative thing to remember is to be gentle with yourself. You might think you don't have anything to forgive yourself for and that may be true, but if you think there might be some work to do, but have no idea where to start, think first of many areas of life you feel guilt, shame or remorse about ANYTHING. That, my friend, is an excellent place to start. If it feels too overwhelming to begin or you are having trouble pinpointing anything in particular. Here are some examples, and side note after the initial forgiveness of self. I believe we greatly benefit by forgiving ourselves on a weekly, monthly, even daily basis *hell maybe even moment to moment*. Start with forgiveness for not being perfect, whatever standard of this you created in your mind, or making "mistakes", or doing or behaving in ways that didn't hold you in the highest light. For eating the damn cheeseburger, I know that may sound ridiculous but for some, even something seemingly insignificant can bring on a whole mental war, of shoulds, shouldnt's. So do yourself a favor and STOP should-ing that crap out of yourself! Here is a list of some of the shame loops that some experience on a regular basis. Feel free to make a list of your own.

I ate the cookies – now I feel like crap – I'm so stupid, and weak, I bet so and so doesn't ever mess up like this!

I make crappy choices in men – I should have known better – my gut told me, speaking of a gut, I shouldn't have eaten those cookies, I'm so dumb!

I wish I had her life. I bet its perfect, and she probably does everything right!

And after writing your list try reading it to yourself in the mirror, if that is too much, start by just reading it aloud. And if that is still too much, thinking it to yourself or writing it out is equally impactful. Whichever way resonates best with you.

I _____ forgive myself for _____, knowing I was doing the best I knew how, and I take the lessons and wisdom gained through this experience and release any harmful residue said circumstance has left in my mind, body, and spirit. So, it is! Repeat this statement verbally or by writing it out or both as many times as necessary. Or you can write yourself or anyone else you forgive a letter, and once you let it all out burn it *in a safe place of course.*

Think about how many times on any given day we can and have the opportunity to make amends to and with ourselves, because left unchecked it will lead to a tireless loop of shame, guilt, and mental exhaustion. Letting go of the un-forgiveness in our hearts towards ourselves helps us facilitate trust from within, make healthier more mindful decisions, and enables us to operate from and show up in the world from a place of confidence and ownership of one's POWER! Not only is that POWERFUL, it is BEAUTIFUL, but it is also EMPOWERING, and it is IMPACTFUL!

You get the idea. We can forgive ourselves for "mistakes" of the past, for old hurts, the way we speak internally to ourselves about ourselves. The list can go on forever *the mind can be relentless* if we let it run wild. Take your time. You are doing great. You are perfect. There is no one else like you. You are doing a fantastic job, and you are enough. Let the rest go so you can move more fluidly through life. Letting go of the burdens of yesterday, fears of tomorrow, and guilt of today. Let it go!

And above all through the healing of forgiveness, you can now view your past in a more loving light, having gone through the process of lifting and digging up, getting to the root of the matter and begin to plant new seeds for a more fruitful future!

Layers

The many layers leading inward.

layer
ˈlāər/
noun

plural noun: layers
A sheet, quantity, or thickness of material, typically one of several, covering a surface or body.

No one understood her, the way magical mysteries danced in her head. Or how going within would ignite an inferno in her heart, or simple acts of love could unleash rivers of joy from her eyes. She is a beautiful enigma this I know.

Belinda Julian

U p to this point, we have been discussing a whole lot about the influence of others and imprinted memories. We have acknowledged the gifts of both the *good* and *not so good,* and the effects they created in our current circumstances. Hopefully you're recognizing and releasing the grips the past still has on you. Moving forward, it's going to get very personal as we delve into the many layers of ourselves. I gave the analogy a while back about the addict and non-addict, and now let's take it a little deeper. While many of us grow up with various degrees of religion or other types of structured beliefs, some grow up without any spiritual or religious background. The rest of us may eventually come to a point in our lives *usually triggered by some outside event or circumstance* where we feel the calling to believe in something greater than ourselves. And some operate their whole lives in a small bubble made up of what others created for them about themselves. Let's just get my beliefs, that I stumbled through and to, out of the way. We are all spiritual beings period and we are having a human experience. In my opinion, we are all the same. We are all PERFECT! We come here already having everything we could ever need or want within us. And as we toil along our journeys we get pretty *banged around.* We begin to forget our inherent greatness *our highest selves.* Then, when we realize we aren't living our most authentic versions of ourselves, we begin to search, and that little voice, starts getting impatient and beckons us to return to ourselves, to the truths we know deep within but have either forgotten or buried. For some this may show up as deepening or strengthening your relationship with spirit. And for others, including myself, it was a search for spiritual meaning and recognizing the divine in myself, others and EVERYTHING. Again, some may get tripped up on certain beliefs. I don't believe it need be a specific person or what any particular religious structure tells you to believe. Rather, it can be a personal relationship, however you believe it to be. As I mentioned before, I believe everyone eventually deepens the already established bond between self and one's higher power. Or they search to know themselves on a deeper level than ever before through something greater than the self. However, you get there, in my opinion, doesn't matter, whether it's god, the universe, higher self, or all of the above. It will look different for everyone, but the call will be the same. And awakening you have is most likely long overdue. Awakening to your truth! Shedding all the parts of you that aren't you, and never were. Showing up in the world in your perfection *self-love*. But before we get super excited and start running towards the sunset. Unless you're are already there, then who am I to stop you? Otherwise, keep on reading! Keep loving and tending to your many layers, not others but your own. We've all heard the term self-love, or "you need to love yourself before you can love anyone else". Maybe you're like me and thought that sounds dandy and great - ok I do love myself! But what does that love look like? Is it surface level? Is it dependent upon others' acceptance of you? Maybe like many it's conditional upon when you are at a certain pinnacle of success, be it physically, financially, or otherwise. If you're anything like me, you've pondered what it really FEELS like, not just looks like, or tried to understand it and live it on an intimate level. Let's look at first some things it is not.

COMPARISON: This is a tough one, especially in our social media-drenched society. The act of comparing ourselves to others is soul-crushing, and might I add based entirely on illusion. It's utterly unrealistic to compare our lives to someone's *highlights* not knowing what the *outtakes* look like. And then to base our mental beat down of ourselves on the partial truth of someone else's life. The truth is many of us do this. And it's is not entirely based on social media, *I think that has just amplified it for some.* I remember years back seeing all the girls on Facebook who had the "perfect" boyfriends, husbands, etc. Meanwhile, I would be brewing a hate stew for whatever guy I was with at the time for not being like that only to find out later said girls with *the perfect mates* broke up, along with the illusions they created. Before anyone gets too worked up, I think social media is great; I am just giving examples of the modern-day struggles. A comparison doesn't only start or end with others. The comparison trap can even be with yourself how you used to look, what you used to do, be, feel and so on. It can be helpful for assessing where you are and where you are going, but I don't recommend it being a focal point for the mental barrage it will sometimes bring. My point being, we all have the journeys that are perfect to advance us along our paths, and they will be vastly different than those around us. We all have our stuff that has shaped and given us form, whatever that may be, and everything is unfolding just as it should. You are perfect the way you are and are the only one in the world like you! *Unless you have a twin!* Joking. You would still be the only one like you. So, do yourself a favor and bask in your own damn glory, you magnificent being you!

Once you move past the comparison trap you can move on to the next layer of loving yourself, hopefully forgiving yourself and others, and repeating as often as necessary. Keep in mind self-love, along with your own becoming *spiritual journey*, is a continual body of work, a journey and not a destination. But loving yourself makes the ride that much smoother and more manageable. Which brings me to how we speak about ourselves to ourselves. Most of this negative nonsense takes place inside our monkey mind but can also spill over to the words we speak about numero Uno, even if it's only in a joking manner. Because how we think, and speak about ourselves, effects how we FEEL about ourselves. So, what are some things you say to yourself or about yourself either in your mind or out loud? We already covered forgiving yourself for past experiences or "mistakes." Hopefully, you are putting that into practice. Aside from those, there is self-care which is something we will delve into later. But to truly love one's self is something a little more difficult to explain because love looks, and more importantly feels, and is experienced differently for everybody. You can start by thinking of someone you love unconditionally. How do you feel when you think about them? What are some things you admire about them? How do you speak about them when they aren't with you? Take it a step further and write a list of these attributes. When you finish, give it a good look because just like the mirror of others reflecting things we don't really like about ourselves, the same mirror reflects back to us our beauty, our strength, our resilience and all the other magic you see in others. We wouldn't even be able to see it if it weren't a part of us as well. This is an excellent place to start. It will be nearly impossible to monitor all of your thoughts but just start observing them. You can begin with noticing yourself thinking or saying things you wouldn't think or say about this person in your life that means so much to you. And start replacing these with the words of adoration you have for your dear beloved. Now we can move into affirmations. Once you're aware of the thoughts and language you use towards yourself, you can start replacing it with more positive words or phrases. This might feel pretty strange at first, but with consistency and persistence, it will start feeling more and more true. Once the feelings accompany what you are affirming, you will gradually notice the things you are thinking and saying becoming your actuality. If you have never read anything by Louise Hay I highly recommend you doing so. I would start with You Can Heal Your Life. That book was an incredible catalyst for me and to be honest probably the reason I got the idea for this book. But as with The Secret, I had to tweak it a little to fit for me *at least initially*. Probably because it blew my mind, but in such an incredibly uplifting way. Maybe you have or have not read it, or something similar. Perhaps the notion of affirmations is completely foreign territory for you; it doesn't matter. We are affirming things to ourselves on a constant basis. I always struggle with, I'm ugly, too old, too skinny, too fat, unlovable, it's essentially turning the things we think or speak around, spinning it in a more positive, productive *true* light. It's weeding out the conditioning of our experiences, or that of, our family, or society that has been fed into our psyche. We then internalized it as our truth. It is not even close to resembling our truth, and usually couldn't be further away from it. These meaning affirmations can work not only with self-love but pretty much anywhere in our lives from finances, to relationships, and so on. But for now, we will stick with self. And here's the thing, I'm all about faking it till you make it *I have done this a ton in my life* you might have to do this a teensy bit; I find with affirmations it's best to start slow and build on it. Let's say you are depressed or in shame, even hate with yourself. Saying "I love myself so deeply and unconditionally" might feel false to you, just rolling off of you like a water droplet on a leaf, not permeating your core in the least. Maybe starting with I have beautiful eyes, or any other positive attributes you can focus on that rings true for you. And like any muscle building exercise, you build strength and endurance with time and consistency. Whatever you do or wherever you start, do it with a grateful heart. Some things

I like to do is say a few affirmations to myself in the morning before I rise, really setting the intention for the day of loving myself. And then simple ways throughout the day, like when I'm ready to jump in the shower first taking a look at myself in the mirror and saying out loud or sometimes just to myself, I Love you! I am beautiful! I am strong! I am sexy, whatever I am feeling, or feeling in need of, for the day. Or it can be during the shower, being grateful and affirming and thanking my strong legs for carrying me through life, or my feet for helping me move through life gracefully. So, as you see it could be simple or more complex but I find two things.

1. Starting with affirming things you believe *of a positive nature* even if it's just a little bit. Then building from there to things you want to believe on a deep soul level. Discarding old beliefs with new more true core beliefs.
2. Starting a statement with I AM, is incredibly powerful.

You can do any variation, even writing lists to yourself filled with I AM….
You can post little notes in your home, car, or at work to remind you.
I am Love
I AM beautiful
I AM powerful
I AM more than enough

If you have trouble saying or believing, or even coming up with affirmations, you can do a quick internet search for ideas picking ones that feel, or that they could feel right to you with a little work. If it's hard for you to believe anything good about yourself in the present moment, you could start by having a trusted friend or family member write a list of some of the things they love or admire about you; maybe even swapping and doing it for each other. All the while knowing the beauty and perfection you see in one another lives inside you, otherwise it would not, could not, be reflected. As long as you keep loving and working and tending to your many beautiful layers, trimming away the old and allowing your true essence to shine, you are well on your way to loving all the incredible facets of yourself. These are just some suggestions as self-love is not definable and most definitely has no finish line. It is only a decision to show up for yourself time and time again, and being your own damn cheerleader! Your personal best friend, and the love of your life. However, that FEELS for you.

Appointment

*Setting aside the time to nurture your mind,
body, and spirit.
Self-care and acts of self-love.*

ap•point•ment
ə'pointmənt/
noun

An arrangement to meet someone at a particular time and
place.

Barren trees surrounded, reminding me that sometimes when we feel we no longer have anything left in us to give. We are just in a gestation period of rest and rejuvenation, and that too is necessary.

Belinda Julian

In continuing the topic of self-love. We will move into self-care, it is just as imperative and genuinely goes hand in hand with loving yourself. Again, this will look entirely different for most, depending on what brings you joy and helps refuel your tank. For a lot of us, this can be a foreign concept, whether that's because you are a parent, a wife, a husband, a working professional, or all of the above. Or someone like me who had been on the co-dependent train, for far too long, consumed with other people's woes, all the while completely neglecting my own. It took a while before I was able to even recognize the yearnings of my soul, all the things my mind, body, and spirit desperately needed. I also know that, for so many, they think they don't have the time to cater to themselves. I would have to disagree strongly. Insert the old analogy of being on a troubled flight, how you must first put the oxygen mask on yourself if you are to be of any help to anyone because if you don't have oxygen, you are dead and can't do a whole lot to help anyone else. So, if it feels a little strange or selfish to cater to yourself, or like you will be neglecting those around you, remember this:

1. You are most likely in dire need of yourself!
2. Know You cannot give from an empty cup. Well you can for a while, but eventually everyone involved will be die of thirst.
3. Know that if your passion is helping or doing for others, you will be able to show up more entirely and unconditionally when you are operating from the overflow of your full cup enabling you to better share your valuable self with others.

What does caring for yourself look like? Note this can be subject to change any given day, month, year or moment. For example, years ago I thought I was fueled by surrounding myself with others.

Now I realize a large percentage of that was me seeking validation outside of myself, equating being overly extended to those around me with feeling important and needed. Now, while being around others fills me to a certain extent, it's after I have, *hermit-ed* my version of going within that I feel most fulfilled. Nowadays I find that time alone in solitude reconnecting with myself is what best renews me the majority of the time, and allows me to listen to the rhythm of my soul and my higher self. When I was so damn busy, I couldn't hear or feel any of it. But for the sake of balance and maintaining my equilibrium it is equally important to spend some quality time around valued friends, and family. On that note, if others around you are used to you giving every last speck of yourself, the call for boundaries will be in order, because sometimes when those around us sense we are changing or evolving it scares them because its new and they don't know what to expect. They are used to how we have been. Or they selfishly want to keep you their personal servant, therapist, maid, etc. and they see your growth as threatening the cozy, little arrangements they have with you. Maybe you are just genuinely filled to the brim busy. You can start with only five to ten minutes alone to do whatever will bring you peace and a little slice of joy. It can be anything reading your favorite magazine, a hot shower or bath, journaling, meditation, taking extra time to do your makeup or hair. The important thing is you commit to whatever seems manageable to you. It could even be just treating yourself for no reason at all; buying flowers for yourself, or having a slice of cake or glass of wine. Hell, it can even be as simple as just taking extra time to exfoliate and moisturize extra good. As a matter of fact, the more things you incorporate and then take the moments to bask in the joy these little treasures bring, dwelling in gratitude for how awesome you feel, the more it becomes a habit and ultimately a way of being for you. The best part of all is that once you start cherishing and nourishing yourself the way you deserve, people around you will naturally follow suit. You will be emitting and most importantly ALLOWING others to reciprocate the love and care you are so graciously giving to yourself. This, by default, allows you to receive which nourishes you in the same way. Receiving can be difficult for a so many, especially the nurturers and givers of the world who don't feel worthy or deserving. The more you give to yourself, the more you send the message to others, and the universe that you are open to receive the abundance of love, affection, and everything else you desire that is ready and waiting to come into your existence. Now doesn't that sound incredible? Start with something, anything small, and build upon it. Before you know it, you will realize it is as necessary as the air you breathe. You will crave your presence, and the gift of your own time and attention, adding more and more to your self-care rituals. Maybe instead of ten minutes, you start adding an hour once or twice a week to take yourself to lunch or read a book in a park or at the beach. There is no limit to the time frames or activities you choose! Whatever you do, try to stay out of the guilt trap, knowing you are tending to your wellbeing and enabling yourself to show up as your best self. We all know how the ego, or what I call the monkey mind, works. As much as others who are dependent on you may try to make you feel guilty, your ego will most likely also try to keep you, small, hidden, or tied to shame and guilt. This is the whole purpose of the ego. By ego I mean what is not us, it is our learned behaviors. The ego fights vehemently to keep things the same, and in the loop of self-sabotage, and self-judgment. It's all the things centered around our false self that is genuinely why at times in our lives we feel such disharmony within. It is because we are at war with our ego mind and our purest self, our soul. We will inevitably feel the tug of war between what our soul knows we are here to experience; which is love, abundance, connection, and wholeness and what our ego has already made up about our experience and lack thereof. It is hell bent to keep us on the hamster wheel of the same old circle of lack, fear, and separateness. So be like the little old ladies with their standing hair *appointments* and continue to give yourself the gift of self-love, self-acceptance, and self-care, no matter who or what tries to stand in the way. Especially, if that person is you.

Double-booked

Slowing down and maintaining balance.

dou•ble
ˈdəb(ə)l/
adjective

Consisting of two equal, identical, or similar parts or things.

book
bo͝ok/
verb

Past tense: booked; past participle: booked

In the stillness of my breath
I AM free.

Belinda Julian

S peaking of the ego mind. There is a duality of light and dark that exists within all of us and the split mind it creates. A sense of separateness internalized within. As we have been discussing so far, maybe not in so many words, we are always evolving, shedding old parts of ourselves and not so much as adding new, but more so personifying and bringing to the fore the truest aspects of ourselves. The layers being shed like petals on a flower exposing deeper into the body that houses our soul. I think I have for the majority of my life been someone who has pondered the duality of all things, and you could even say that sometimes it has been both a blessing and a curse. A blessing because of the empathy I can display for others. And at times a curse for the same reason because I have been able to see the light in even some of the darkest people. It has at times led me a bit too deep with others trying to hold my mirror to show them the light in themselves when they weren't ready or capable of even looking at the reflection in front of them. But as we know nothing is wasted and this, of course, all helped me decipher how to see and keep the light within myself aglow while simultaneously learning how to give to others in need of light without leaving myself completely burnt out and in the dark. I think that is the purpose of life, to discard all that keeps our light hidden, and once we learn how to do that to share our light with others. Which leads me to one of the quickest most efficient ways to start tapping into your inner light. Meditation. There is no quicker route to spark a conversation with your soul and tap into your unlimited potential; especially if you have for far too long been estranged from yourself. I think many people never start because they think meditating has to look or feel a certain way, leading them to give up before they even had a chance to start. I have had many different *interesting* and highly enlightening experiences meditating that looked and felt nothing like what I had expected. I remember anticipating that I must sit in complete silence, maybe chant some oms and POOF some euphoric feeling would consume me, and I would be well on my way to becoming the next Deepak Chopra. Like many things in my life, my expectations were dramatically different from my reality and much more an evolution, not at all the limited notions made up by me of it being only a particular way. The most important being that my meditation practice has been very much a journey, no two times are the same, but all are what I need at the moment. That's the beauty and perfection of the workings of divine timing. What you need always shows up even if it looks vastly different than what you expect.

Ok, so speaking of Deepak Chopra, that is how I was first introduced to meditation. He and Oprah have these free twenty-one-day meditation series they offer that they created together. A friend had emailed me the link to the sign in, and I was on my way to start this incredible journey. There is some talking in the beginning, and then you are led to a guided meditation. If I remember, from start to finish is about twenty minutes which is super manageable and not overwhelming at all. It's as if you have someone holding your hand through it, rather than trying and "failing" to just shut your thoughts off completely all by yourself. As some of you may know, that has the complete opposite effect. As soon as you even think of having no thoughts, it's almost as though your brain gets the opposite message, immediately bombarding you with a whole onslaught of ridiculous and irrelevant thoughts. By no means were my thoughts completely shut off, but I did experience small interludes of nothingness and might I add, overall a more relaxed state. Continuing from there I started listening to guided meditations from YouTube, just a simple search and there are millions to choose from, I would pick themed ones whether it was balancing chakras, healing your inner child, or just plain and simple relaxation recordings. Here's the thing, most of the time I would fall asleep, waking as soon as it was over, which of course was not at all what I expected, but I know now to be exactly what I needed. After all, I was healing years of stored trauma in my psyche. To this day I still enjoy guided meditations, and find myself returning to old faithful's, but these days I find more often than not just sitting in solitude when I feel that I am in need of some time out, a reset, or in need of guidance. *IN THE STILLNESS OF MY BREATH I AM FREE.* During this I still may not be completely void of thought but rather in a place of just observing thoughts mindlessly until they settle, then I am clear and centered for guidance or whatever I may need at the moment. And yes sometimes it might just be a nap. Never underestimate the healing power of a good nap. Whatever it is that comes to you, as long as you allow it, being mindful not to judge it.

Speaking of allowing and what you need coming to you, another experience I would have sometimes while in meditation would be a spinning sensation, if you have ever been drunk and had the spins or had vertigo, imagine that times a hundred. Anytime this would happen I would immediately get anxious and open my eyes. It wasn't until working with a life coach and we were doing some powerful and intense healing work through meditation that this happened again, this time instead of just opening my eyes and avoiding in it. I stayed with it and let me tell you it was terrifying but what I felt *and knew* at the time in the eye of the storm was that it was necessary. I could feel that it was complete and utter fear that I was moving through, clearing the energy out of my body and mind. I don't know if I could ever really accurately describe it, and I might be scaring the crap out of you making you never try meditation or to ever continue with your practice. But the point is how insanely powerful our mind, and the fear that can be housed there, is. Not to mention the energy, trauma, and stored wounds of our pasts. I especially experienced this because I had avoided, blocked out, numbed out so much that had hurt me. You see the dark aspects of us are always waiting and really only want to be brought into the light to be observed, acknowledged and healed. That is precisely what happened and continues to happen for me through the power of meditation. After the initial moving through the fear in my time of meditation, I had a handful of times where I would feel the need to rest, and would close my eyes and experience the spinning again and instead of going to fear I just relaxed into it and as it changed in intensity and direction I could feel that my energy center, or chakras were being balanced and cleansed ultimately leaving me feeling relaxed, grounded and centered.

Now, I hope I didn't scare the crap out of you about meditation, when I really just intended to make a point that there is no cookie cutter, or black and white version of meditation. Each individuals practice will look and feel completely different, but the benefits will be similar in the way of you being more relaxed, centered, in touch with your inner self, not to mention the soul level healing that can and will take place. So, what do you say? How about you give it a whirl? If you are completely new to meditation. Whatever it is you are desiring whether its decreasing stress, taking time to connect with yourself, going within for answers, adding to your self-care/self-love practice, or healing your mind, body and spirit or any combination of all of these.

Some suggestions:

Spending at least 10 minutes in quiet solitude up to however long you'd like, or can manage.

Try a guided meditation. I used YouTube mostly, but whatever works for you, whether you buy a favorite cd, or download an app, or rent from the library.

Plenty of people enjoy a walking meditation. First start by picking a place in nature that brings you tranquility such as a park, near a body of water, etc. walking in a slow, steady pace being mindful of your breath, and staying present in your body.

Another simple way to ground yourself in the present moment through meditation is just sitting or spending time in nature.

All of these of course are just suggestions. As my Pilates instructor always says, "it's your practice." So, have fun with it, try different methods and find your fit. Above all be patient, enjoy from a detached perspective and aim for consistency to avoid being *double-booked* and the possible burnout, it will bring.

Consultation

Seeking and receiving outside help.

con•sul•ta•tion
ˌkänsəlˈtāSH(ə)n/
noun

The action or process of formally consulting or discussing.

We spoke briefly about being open to receiving, and sometimes this includes receiving help from sources or people outside of ourselves. Having acknowledged now that what shapes us does not have to define us, that the bricks that life dealt us are only building blocks to create a life of abundance and purpose. And the adage, *it takes a village*, not just in raising children, but in raising us to the heights we wish to achieve. At times, this means reaching out for healing help. Rather than reaching out externally to numb ourselves with toxic and addictive behaviors although we are human. *I think we all have done this from time to time, even if it's just drowning in a bag of Cheetos.* Ultimately though, in the extreme versions *insert ex-boyfriend* or me helping everyone but myself. We are just pushing the inner work to the side, keeping wellness and peace at bay. For many reasons, we don't know how to cope; it's too painful, we've blocked it out, possibly not even realizing what we are numbing out. I remember around the age of eighteen, all of a sudden feeling this constant heaviness in my chest, feeling as though I couldn't breathe, and as I was telling my friend about it, and she said, "It sounds like you have anxiety." I was relieved to be able to put a name to what I was experiencing but had no idea what to do with this revelation or how or where the hell it came from; but I knew for sure I didn't want to continue to feel that way. After exploring my options, one being medication which I did not want to take, I barely like taking Advil. I decided to go to therapy. I knew that I thought about things all the time *racing thoughts* but didn't realize or recognize it as stress. I always had kind of just systematically forgiven and dismissed things that had happened to me as a way of survival, never taking my feelings and emotions into account. And naively, I thought I was just thinking about things not stressing about them, not knowing the effects the mind has on the body and how when things need attention they will sometimes show up as physical manifestations in our body.

Off to therapy, I went, realizing after surviving a handful of chaotic years that I needed to heal in the post-traumatic aftermath. These symptoms of anxiety happened many times throughout my life in all sorts of different forms; a heavy chest, full-blown panic attacks, heart palpitations, just to name a few, After working through all those, I still frequently had an overall feeling of unease. Going to therapy on and off through the years, tons of self-help books, a few seminars and recently working relentlessly to heal internally, but still experiencing what some would call a dark night of the soul. It's the struggle of the death of the ego; *also looks a lot like depression.* Being stuck between the split mind in the most severe of ways. Your soul is calling you forth, but the ego is keeping you bound to the past. Keeping you stagnant: and for you to truly move forward, you must experience the death of ego *leaving behind all that you previously believed to be true.*

Even though it technically is a beautiful thing IN HINDSIGHT, at the time, it can be very confusing; When you are being called to rise above and move forward but are dragging the shackles of the past, you reach a point where that is no longer an option. This lead me to work with a life coach, because even though I had achieved so much inner transformation, and awareness, there were still some blocks holding me back. I was having a hard time moving past them and needed help to get over the last leg of this particular journey. This was incredibly hard, considering I'm generally a do-it-yourselfer. But nonetheless, putting my ego aside had to be one of the best decisions I have ever made. Ok so again, I may be freaking everyone out, and you might be saying forget this inner work crap, it sounds terrible. Just remember:

1. Not everyone will have to dig and gut out as much. But my point of all of this was that when you are embarking on the road of inner transformation, it is ok and highly recommended to invite some company along for the ride, it will make it a whole lot less lonely, and a hell of a lot less scary.
2. Although some personally view getting or receiving help as a form of weakness or think it is strange or weird, it will, in fact, help you tremendously on the road to inner freedom.

I cannot tell you how many people over the years I suggested therapy to *gently of course* who all probably wanted to punch me in the throat. Lucky for me no one ever did. They must have sensed it was coming from a loving place and not at all condescending. I'll never forget having a conversation with a friend of mine and telling her how much therapy helped me at different times in my life. And she said, "Isn't it weird, you just go tell a stranger all of your secrets?". Even if you don't have tons to work through, sometimes it is even nice just to go and feel heard, or understood. Or like I told my friend "yes, it is sort of exactly like that. You go and unload all of the 'baggage' you are carrying around, and you leave it there l making you feel lighter, literally and figuratively".

Or perhaps you are or have just gone through some hard times or something especially challenging. And you are tired or feel as though you are overwhelming your friends and family with your troubles, or you feel like they are tired of hearing about it, or you just don't want to bother them, but you still need to process it some more. It is incredible to have an unbiased professional to bounce things off of, to gain some perspective, and have a safe place to lay down your burdens. It's being able to unload the millions of thoughts and stories running rampant in your mind, even if only for the hour. All of this, therapy, coaches, books, seminars, retreats, podcast, etc. are all another layer of self-care. The more we can work on weeding out the *negative* and replace with *positive* the more it becomes second nature. All of the shadow work takes time and consistent effort, and it takes tremendous courage and strength to be vulnerable enough to let others help guide or walk you through something. Being vulnerable took me a long while to learn, I thought I always have had to be this pillar of strength. I learned it wasn't strength at all. It was fear!

Being transparent and feeling exposed can be a terrifying place. But when you build that personal trust and learn to listen to your intuition, it can seem a little less daunting. You may falter, or make a "mistake." You may get hurt, or travel partially in the "wrong" direction; but know every step you take towards yourself no matter how minute it seems, is a step closer to living an authentic life. A life you feel great about, and that gives you more and more to be grateful for, knowing you can expect great things. The way I see it, you only have things to gain.

So, have a good lengthy consultation with yourself. What do you need? An inspiring podcast in the morning to liven up your day and help you stay inspired? Do you feel a little directionless and a life coach could help you have more structure in your life? Is there a yoga or spiritual retreat you have been longing to go on? It could just be getting together with a fantastic group of friends and sharing about your lives. Wherever you find yourself, please just bring all the softness and vulnerability you can. There is real magic there. When you operate from this sweet spot, a whole new world will open up and rise to meet you. Doesn't that sound amazing?

Colored

Taking the time to Color outside of the lines;
Envisioning and creating your dream life.

col•ored
ˈkələrd/
adjective

Having or having been given color or colors, especially as
opposed to being black, white, or neutral.

When one begins or has some sort of spiritual awakening its generally because they realize that;

A. things aren't working, causing them to search for higher meaning.
B. Something traumatic happens, forcing them to seek a higher meaning.
C. They get tired of their own B.S.
D. All of the above.

My point being, that some grow up being taught that greatness, love, abundance, success, and possibility are to be expected and are somewhat inevitable. Others, are repeatedly shown that they are small and should not aspire to anything greater. Neither one is an example of what is easier or harder. Because you can hold either of those beliefs no matter what your experience has been. Eventually there is a call to shed all the outdated beliefs, all that doesn't serve you, and step forward to a new way of being. Maybe you've had the wake-up calls or the prompts for a new way of being, part of that being living life in your full authenticity and living a life of purpose, or living a life of passion. Let's put the passion on ice, and focus on purpose, as you can and will have many passions throughout your life. And some people tend to get overwhelmed with the idea of finding their passion.

You are probably thinking the same can be said for finding or living a life of purpose. A lighter way to approach it would be to think about what intentionally living a purposeful life might look, and most importantly, feel like? Gone are the days of being a passive participant in your life, believing that life is just happening to you. But rather, knowing that when you are tapped into your spirit and in communication with your soul, you realize that life is happening for you in all ways and at all times. So, what's next, you might ask? Well, keep falling in love with yourself on a daily basis; make the time to invite more of the intimate conversations between you and your higher soul-self. Spend less time listening to the monkey mind. Then start following the breadcrumbs, and the more you follow them you will begin to *figure it out* for yourself.

It doesn't have to be some massive revelation like you're going to be the next Gandhi. It could just be you want to live a life with more peace in your heart, have more time to engage in creative pursuits, or want a life that allows you to travel the world. The idea being, now is the time to start thinking, imagining, visualizing what your ideal life will look like, and how it will make you feel. What is the feeling you want? You don't need to have all the answers right away, or ever, really, just as long as you are moving. Even if it's only in your mind, for now.

The most important thing is BELIEF that a magnificent life filled with everything you ever wanted is yours for the taking. You are worthy enough, and far more capable than you know or that others have believed you to be. All you need is a little seed, a small kernel of hope. That's all it takes. That's the way this all happened for me and how this book even came to be. First, as you are well aware, was the acknowledgment of how my life was not working for me. Each challenge better prepared me for the next, and also taught me explicitly, all the things I *didn't* want.

I started following the crumbs, which at first was just a call to do something impactful. Next, was healing the deep wounds, while simultaneously having the intense desire to find meaning and establish love as I'd never known with myself. And because I have always been drawn to all things esoteric, I enjoyed searching and gathering new information and insight for myself. I immersed myself in all sorts of different teachings, readings, things that were metaphysical and spiritual by nature, with a ferocity I'd never experienced before. When I started asking myself the next set of questions, why am I here? What am I supposed to be doing with this calling I was feeling? And what the heck did any of it mean?

And then, one day I'll never forget, I can still feel it and see it with such clarity. I was sitting on my porch, my cat in my lap, the sun shining on my face, and feeling the closest I had ever been to being in a meditative state. I was just observing my thoughts, trying to feel my way to which direction I was being urged to move toward; as I went down the line; should I open a wellness center; become a life coach; open a metaphysical store? None of which resonated with me. Then BAM! All of a sudden, I pictured myself writing a book *something I had never even considered*. I saw myself being part of Oprah's book club, being a best-selling author, being published by a particular publishing house. I also visualized myself doing book signings, and felt myself signing the books one by one. It was like nothing I had ever experienced.

About an hour later I was on my way to work, and my mind was still processing everything. Thoughts spun around in my head such as I don't know how the hell to write a book; I didn't even go to high school; I don't know what the heck I would write, or who would read it if I did. My thoughts were swirling like, do I have anything valuable to say, blah, blah, blah, you know how the mind is, working itself into a tailspin.

Well, when I arrive at work about an hour later and my boss lets me know I have a difficult client ready for me. I put on the full charm, trying as best I can to get her to soften up, which of course she does. And as I am cutting her hair I'm asking her all the typical questions to get to know her and her lifestyle a little better. Then she begins to tell me she is writing a book. She goes on to say how she has just been journaling her weight loss journey and so on. So, I asked her if it just for her or does she plan to have it published? When she says, "Oh I want to be published with so and so the same exact publishing house I just visualized, *insert me internally freaking out*. Now I don't know if she did, or will do that, as I've never seen her again. But I got the message, loud and clear!

I mean even if you don't believe in signs or serendipitous moments, it was hard not to feel in some way that this was a definite sign! Maybe if my intense visualization had happened days, months or years earlier I could have just passed it off. But come on now, when the universe speaks to you so freaking obviously, you cannot help but take notice. And notice I did, messages were coming in fast and furiously. About a day or two later while driving, the book's title and chapter ideas came to me in a flash of inspiration. It left me with the outline of a book I never knew I wanted to write and had absolutely no idea how to construct. But I just keep listening and following each breadcrumb.

My point is, if you have the belief, and the determination to follow whatever it is you feel calling you, life will meet you there, and encourage you along the way. All you have to do is start a conversation with yourself. Your soul knows far more than anything you could ever conjure up in your mind. Be still. Be patient, and it will come. This combined with faith, trust, and self-belief, and you will be unstoppable. The sky is indeed the limit. What do you say? Today is a great day to start *coloring* outside of the lines, all of the lines that have kept you boxed in playing small, all the lines that have confined you be it societal, familial, environmental. Leave behind a life based on the confines of your experiences.

Now is the time to get bold, get expansive in creating *even if only in your mind, for now* a life much grander than your life thus far. A life more fulfilling than you can even comprehend. A life vastly different than anything you ever thought possible, until now. You can do it, and you deserve it. And don't forget to have fun with it. Don't stress or try to figure it all out in a day, just relax into the flow, and let it all come to you. You've got this! Side note, if you need a little help igniting the stream, a few things I've found that really help me tap in are:

Intention setting:

I love setting intentions! I do it every year *New Year* rather than having resolutions, I like to create a list of my intentions for the year. It instantly takes the pressure off and sheds the guilt of possibly not succeeding at resolutions. Instead it lets the universe know your visions for yourself. I do this for the year the more significant things, for the month, and even the week or day by day. The key is to just write it down, and sort of forget about it. Don't keep checking it every day as you've already sent it out to the universe. Trust that it will all come to fruition. You can check every so often, just to be amazed at how many things you can check off as they happen effortlessly. As long as you are not in resistance to that which you are calling into your life, there is no option other than for it to show up in your life. A great exercise to practice starts with simple intentions that aren't really of great importance, and that you aren't tied to in any way. For example, one day I did this after it was recommended by my life coach, and I wrote.

1. See someone I haven't seen in years.
2. Have someone buy me a meal
3. Receive unexpected money.

I almost completely had forgotten about my list. When a few days later I found it, and realized I had gotten an unexpected extra six hundred dollars in child support, I ran into an old friend I hadn't seen in probably ten years, and a friend of mine brought me a slice of pizza and salad, just because. All this within a couple of days. I mean WHOA! You see when you start small and lessen your resistance and start seeing results, and like any muscle, over time you start building your intention setting power. Pretty cool stuff! Go ahead and try it out for yourself!

Visualizing:

This might not happen spontaneously the way it did for me in the incident I described. But I have used visualization many times. Generally, you want to be in a relaxed, semi-meditative state, and you can just let the images come up authentically. If you are seeking guidance or want to consciously create your vision, get into a relaxed state either on your own or with a guided meditation explicitly geared toward visualizing your ideal life. If it is a particular situation and you desire a specific outcome, sit in that still place picturing in your mind's eye what it would look like, using as many details as possible, and imagine how you will feel. Let's say you have a big meeting and you want it to go a certain way. Visualizing how you would like it to unfold beforehand dramatically aids in things going in your desired direction. Or maybe you want to bring a particular lifestyle or way of being into your reality, believe, envision it with as much clarity as possible and as if it has already happened. This way there is no other option than your reality to follow suit.

Writing:

Writing is just another means of calling in the things you want. I feel when you put pen to paper it really makes things real and really brings them to life. One particularly inspiring exercise is to write a letter to your future self. You choose two, five, or ten years from where you are now, heck even one for each if you are feeling really fired up. Really go in with as many feelings, details, and as much emotion as possible, don't censor yourself. Put anything and everything, from the man/woman of your dreams, your dream home/location, career, and lifestyle. Pay particular attention to how you feel. After all, we usually desire things because we want the feelings we think will go with them. So, start coloring the beautiful vibrant life of your dreams and don't be scared if it is outside the lines. That's where the magic happens!

Highlights

Highlighting the good in your life; having gratitude.

high•light
ˈhīˌlīt/
noun

plural noun: highlights
An outstanding part of an event or period of time.
"he views that season as the highlight of his career."
synonyms: high point, best part, climax, peak, pinnacle, height,
acme, zenith, summit, crowning moment.

Allow love to permeate from your aura,
Shine bright with your smile,
Linger on your every word
And radiate beautifully from your heart.

Belinda Julian

S peaking of the feelings that accompany our desires. There is no quicker way of feeling the effects of this in the present moment. And that is GRATITUDE!

Here's a rule of thumb; the more you feel gratitude, the more you will have to be grateful for. So, when you are setting intentions, visualizing or just yearning for specific desires to come to fruition, it is of equal importance to acknowledge what you are actually seeking. Say you desire a thinner or more fit body. Maybe you would like to see more financial stability/ freedom in your life, or a loving, fulfilling intimate relationship, whatever it is, know you deserve it and are capable of receiving it, whatever it may be. As a matter of fact, you couldn't even hold an intention, desire or dream, if it weren't possible or already yours for the taking. That being said, I would say there are a few different layers at hand here. First in line is.

Gratitude:

Regularly practicing gratitude helps us maintain a healthy perspective, even in the so-called bad times. This does not negate or mean that we are in denial or are ignorant about less than desirable occurrences in our lives, but rather, it helps strengthen our faith muscle. Believing that all is as it should be, and knowing everything is molding us. Spending even just a few moments throughout your day either writing a list of things you are grateful for, silently thinking them to yourself, or saying them aloud, will instantly put you in a better mood, as well as a more receptive mode. I often find when we are in a crap mood it's because we are feeling a lack of something in our lives. I know it sounds cliché, but it can be difficult when we are committed to staying in victim mode, or on the hamster wheel of our stories and struggles. Feeling sorry for ourselves is a default we have been comfortable with for a long time. It is not where we truly belong. I promise you, no matter how void our lives can be of the things we think will make us happy, there is always something to be grateful for. Start small, like a stranger smiled at you, you can walk, talk, have electricity, good health, etc. When you find the many things that are abundant in your life, try to take a moment to really relish how it feels to be so blessed.

When I wake in the morning, I like to spend a few moments just reviewing things I am grateful for. And sometimes I do it throughout the day, just because. As always, the more you do it, the more it becomes the new norm. I know being grateful can be difficult when things aren't going well, but when you practice gratitude on a daily basis, those slumps will be fewer and shorter-lived because eventually, you will be grateful even for those, because you will have an awareness of what and why it is showing up, and your bounce back reflex will be in full effect. You may get down but will no longer be down and out. Which leads me to.

Why:
What are you why's?
You want to be skinnier?
Have more money?
More time?
Better health?

And so on, what feelings do you think having your desires will deliver to you? More security, confidence, feeling sexier. Whatever the feeling is you believe said circumstances will bring, work on feeling that way in the now. If you think being skinnier, wealthier, or healthier, etc. is going to deliver your happiness on a platter and it might, but then it will just be onto the next set of somethings. Thinking xyz will sustain inner contentment will always be short lived. They say, "It's a whole lot more comfortable to cry in a Mercedes than on a bike!"

My roundabout point is while it's fantastic to be a co-creator in your life and you deserve and can have the world, it's equally important to be in the here and now. And feel good now. Otherwise all that which we are seeking, all the abundance in the world will not make us truly, long lastingly happy. Some people seemingly have it all. Take a look at some of the most infamous musicians, actors, millionaires who as far back as history can track, have died from overdoses or suicides, because they lacked inner contentment. Without the foundation of inner peace, self-love, and appreciation, things outside of us will continue to be just that, something always outside of us just dangling outside of our reach, never quite fulfilling, and seemingly unattainable. Which leads me to the next point.

Being receptive:

All that I mentioned before helps put you in the mode of being receptive to all the things you wish to bring into your existence. By removing the blocks that stand in the way of you receiving, by embodying all that you seek, and by being in this space, you naturally and effortlessly will attract your desires, rather than depending on circumstances outside of you to make you feel whole and complete. When you do receive. It will be the icing on top of your already plentiful cake.

I used to, and still do on occasion, get swept up in the desires of tomorrow. And while it is so important and part of our innate nature to be powerful manifestors, visualizing and creating all that we can conjure up in our human minds, there's the sometimes-tricky art of staying in the moment. As we all know, yesterday has already come and gone, and tomorrow is never promised. No matter what greatness we would like to see, or feel in our life, the real magic is being that now! At least getting in the space of feeling the way you imagine you will feel when your desires come to fruition. Although there will always be something we desire in the future, and that is entirely normal, if we get so results oriented we will sometimes not even pause to enjoy the fruits of our labor. And ultimately, what we are genuinely chasing, is the feeling.

So, feel good now! After all, isn't that what we all want? Do you want more abundance in your life? Start relishing the abundance that surrounds you. Don't feel like you can find any? Focus on the simple things, your breath, your freedom, petting your dog or cat, being in nature. Want a better body? Stop trying to guilt and shame yourself into your ideal number, size, tone or shape you cannot hate yourself into being Skinny. Embrace and love who you are now. Dress and do your make up now, as you would at some future date when you think you will finally feel deserving. Thank your strong legs for carrying you through life the same legs you've shamed for various reasons. Thank your stretch marks that created space for your pre-pubescent, or pregnant body be grateful it was able to accommodate space for what you needed.

You want a stable, considerate, devoted partner? Start being that for yourself, start being a living, breathing example of how you deserve to be treated. Show up for yourself the way you want others to. Respect yourself the way you want to be respected. Value yourself exactly where you are. Take yourself on a date, or buy yourself flowers for no damn reason, other than they are beautiful and you like them. When all else fails, take a few deep breaths.

Write a gratitude list.

Spend a few moments thinking of something or someone you are completely grateful for.

Call or tell someone how grateful you are for their support, relationship, and love.

Be out in nature *the speedway to being centered and in the moment*, feeling gratitude for the beauty that surrounds you.

As with everything, build up and work on your ability to focus on the beauty and abundance in your life, rather than live in fear and lack. Every minute you spend making gratitude a way of life for you, the easier it will be to find the beauty and plenty that already surrounds you and all that which is making its way into your life. So, make like a neon marker and start *highlighting!*

Teased

*Sometimes being "shoved" down prepares you
to reach further heights than you ever imagined.*

tease
tēz/
verb

Past tense: teased; past participle: teased
gently pull or comb (something tangled, especially wool or hair)
into separate strands.

Once you are working with all this awareness, and you are in the driver's seat, steering your life in the direction that you want, you may still see a lot that you don't want. This can be when your faith is really tested, and frustration kicks in. A crucial and quite vital lesson is staying in a place of detachment. This can be especially challenging for people like me *control freak*, or the overachievers who feel they have to be DOING all the time.

Detachment, can be a difficult concept to wrap your head around. Much like forgiveness, the challenging hump to get over is thinking it means condoning what has been done, which we know now is furthest from the truth. Similarly, with detachment the actual meaning is the state of being objective or aloof. It's almost as a negative, like you give up, don't care, or are lazy. But in practice, the art of detachment is to SURRENDER our need to control every single detail. To allow the unfolding and TRUST that all is exactly as it should be.

We have our visions. We have our intentions. Yet sometimes, we still need to learn the lesson of ACCEPTANCE and PATIENCE. You might start noticing many things in your life showing up. And sometimes they will be totally different from your desires. To say this can be disheartening and frustrating is an understatement. But I am here to tell you that literally *nothing* is wasted. Each and everything that shows up, even if it is slightly different than what you imagined, is preparing you for what you asked for. Every fork in the road that seems to be a detour is building your faith, your determination, your resolve, and ultimately lighting up your target. There may be some missed shots, but you are just honing your craft.

Trust the process, and as cliché as it sounds, enjoy the journey. Each no is an invitation to delve further into yourself. Each setback is an opportunity to know yourself on a deeper level, and a chance to practice what may be new to you, which is operating in an entirely new way than you have before. You are probably used to trying really hard *our need to control based out of fear*, and now that old operating system no longer works. It's much more about ALLOWING which comes through love and trust. Let's examine these concepts a little closer. When we are making significant changes internally, its inspiring, and vital to have our vision, goals, and desires in mind to use as a compass. Yet we mustn't get so future focused, or end goal focused that there is no room for spontaneity. It's important to know there is divine timing at play, and an unseen team guiding and supporting all of us. Sometimes things don't happen all at once, and most certainly not according to our timeline. Keep in mind the refinement you are always growing into. Most importantly, although you have certain things in mind, many times there is all of that and plenty more awaiting you. And they are bigger and better things than you could ever construct on your own. It is of utmost importance to keep these principles in mind.

Acceptance:

Learning to be ok with where we are right now, finding and acknowledging all the beauty and love that surrounds us at this very moment. Know we are always in the exact place we are meant to be, and there are no mistakes. The goal or point is to really feel peace, happiness, contentment, and love internally. Accepting is everything. This is a difficult one for most, but as with most transformations, it's the place to start. This means acceptance of who you've been, your experiences, your mistakes, all the things you dislike about yourself, and are learning to like. Hopefully you will ultimately learn to love them.

Surrender:

Sometimes when you feel backed into a corner and you've done all you can, do and pushed as hard as you can, this is a huge sign that it is time to surrender to whatever your higher power is. Usually this means there is something you don't see, or something else you need to learn *pause and reflect.* Basically, you have been plugging away *doing* when you really just need to be *being.* I like the saying, "We are human beings, not human doings". We are so used to doing everything and equating productivity with worthiness. We are so afraid to just sit and be, thinking that then things won't happen, or we will miss an opportunity. Or millions of other outdated beliefs. We must learn to go with the flow and know that we are safe.

Trust:

This requires a great deal of faith. Find that place, even if its deep within you, that knows you can trust yourself, others, life, etc. If we have been in many circumstances where we felt we couldn't trust, just take a good long look at how it all has actually worked out regardless of how it felt at the time. You made it through, you learned, and grew and evolved. Most of all you survived. Now you need to trust in yourself to thrive.

Allowing:

Being open and receptive to all the gifts and magic that are waiting to come into your life requires believing you deserve it all. So, don't block the blessings by being closed to the possibilities. How many times have any of us received, or were about to receive, things we really wanted and as soon as we feel the excitement bubbling up we get scared and self-sabotage? Then starts the cycle of viscous self-deprecation, and we slip right back into the old martyr or victim role.

Patience:

And remember sometimes getting shoved down prepares you to rise to greater heights than you could have ever imagined. When life seems to be *teasing* you, just know it is really prepping you for all of your desires and then some.

"You are allowed to be both a masterpiece and a work in progress simultaneously." ~ Sophia Bush

Also, remember to have acceptance of where you have been and where you are now. Surrender to the fact that you are always exactly where you are meant to be. Trust that you are deserving of everything you want and more. Allow yourself to be open to receive all that you desire and then some. I know this concept of patience can be trying, especially now that we are all so accustomed to instant gratification, and having everything just a click away. Believe me, I can be incredibly impatient and have had to re-learn quite a few times the lesson of structure, and discipline, rather than just speeding forward and bypassing all that makes me uncomfortable.

A LOT of times I have found that when I am feeling the most impatient is when I need to stop, pause, and focus on my breath. Last but certainly not least, remember this transformation is not a race. Undoing a lifetime of habits and learned behaviors takes time and is an ongoing process. All the places you long to arrive at, actual and metaphorical, are all waiting and ready for your arrival, in perfect timing. Though at times you may feel you are just being teased, you are really being prepared and prepped for all of your greatest desires and ambitions to unfold beautifully. Perfectly!

Client

We are all both the student and the teacher in the grand classroom we call life.

cli•ent
ˈklīənt/
noun1.

A person or organization using the services of a lawyer or other professional person or company.

Beauty is all the things that tried to break you but actually made you stronger.
It's a loving embrace.
It is the essence we see in others that we sometimes fail to recognize in ourselves.
Beauty is the courage to keep putting one foot in front of the other no matter how bad we want to run in the other direction.
Beauty is the excitement of new beginnings.
Knowing we are all in this together.

Belinda Julian

M uch like the mirrors that reflect back to us some of the considerable activity going on within ourselves, once aware of the significant things at play in our lives, we can begin to get in tune with the subtler cues that are constantly alive and at work. We are always both the student and the teacher. Being the student, we continuously are gifted with the opportunity to see what is going on internally, by what is happening externally around us. And being the teacher, we are able to be a real-life example of living in our truth, and guiding others to do the same. All the things that others stir up inside us, or *trigger* internally, give us the beautiful gift of searching deeper within. The person that annoys you because they are judgmental is an opportunity to check in with how you are perhaps judgmental too. The friend that you get frustrated with because they aren't living up to their full potential gives you the chance to look at ways you can start making changes that are aligned with your higher path.

The delays and stalls that continually surround you, let you know it is time to pause, reflect, and focus on your breath and being in the moment. All of these are like *lesson plans* in the classroom we call life. Some of these lessons include how we REACT based on our EXPECTATIONS. They are rooted in the many stories we operate from on a regular basis.

How many times have you built up a particular experience and loaded it with expectations, only to be disappointed, hurt, angry or confused? Then we play the blame game. It is their fault I feel this way. If only they would do things a specific way then we would feel better, whole, complete, understood. How many times a day even do you hear those around you venting about the faults of others. And how those people, be it a boss, lover, friend, did such and such, and they are so terrible, etc.,

etc... insert their story about feeling unheard, being the victim, not being valued, whatever it may be. This is where both the good and the bad news comes in. The bad news is, we have no control over what anyone else does. The good news is, we do have control over how we react, to everything people, places, and things. We control how we feel, and get to choose to not take things personally. We always have the choice to decide what our PERSPECTIVE will be, and the lens through which we see things.

While it is excellent to have intentions, and expect the best, expectations, especially when it comes to others behavior or what we think it *should* be, will almost always leave us feeling disappointed.

This means we are entirely in charge of how we feel, and how we react to things. That all may sound pretty harsh, but it is actually a gift to know that we can free ourselves from much unnecessary suffering. We always have the gift of choosing peace and contentment in every single situation in our life. And on a moment to moment basis.

This isn't to say we go through our lives like some sort of zombies. Instead of that, we choose to own our power, and not give it away. We also relinquish others of being *responsible* for our internal space and inner peace. This doesn't mean that tact, compassion, grace, and consideration shouldn't be practiced by all individuals and be the baseline of respect at all times, but rather that we don't take the baggage of others personally. Man, I really wish someone would have told me this years ago. I took everything personally for far too long, and carried it like a badge of honor. This includes the inability of others to value, love, or support me. I took it all as a direct reflection of my worth. It is so important to have a healthy perspective and realistic expectations. It helps to temper our reactions. Let's delve a little deeper.

Perspective:

Whether it is dealing with others or our own set of challenging circumstances, perspective is everything! We can always choose whether our perspective is one rooted in love or fear. Even the most dire of situations can be viewed in a positive light if we make a choice to do so. When we are learning to operate in a new manor, it can be easy to fall back to our default behavior, functioning from a place of lack, fear, blame or scarcity. Momentarily we might resort to our old ways, but once we realize they no longer serve us, and that viewing things from a lighter place is much more beneficial, we can easily transmute negative feelings or thoughts into positive ones.

Expectations:

While it is fantastic to have enormous expectations for yourself and the direction of your life, when it comes to the actions and behavior of others, it is not so black and white. They have their free will, and are only able to meet us where they are at the time. Expecting anything other than who they are in that moment will just disappoint us. However, we can choose to view all parties in a loving, accepting light, void of any preconceived notions of how we think they *should be* or how we think things should play out. In other words, taking others as they are, and respecting their journey, will save everyone involved a lot of unnecessary discomfort.

Reactions:

Which leads me to this in-between place of acceptance and optimism. When our wounds and pain is triggered while interacting with others, we have three options;

1. Know that the negativity being projected onto us has nothing to do with us, and everything to do with the stories and unhealed wounds of the other person. So, don't take it personally.
2. See our role in the situation., Our wounds and stories are being brought into the light so we can feel, understand, and deal with them.
3. Recognize that out of the discomfort of the situation, event, or confrontation healing can arise for all parties.

Once again, these are concepts that develop over time, but with awareness and understanding, they can, and will, significantly affect our inner peace. I know it can be difficult when we are in situations where emotions are intensified, but if you can take anything from this, I would say, to really work on not taking things personally. Communicate as clearly as you can when dealing with others. Ask questions when you need clarification. And remember, we are all constantly learning, so if you can spend more and more time living and feeling peace, you will, by default, diffuse situations that would otherwise be or felt un-peaceful. Moment by moment, you are choosing to remain tranquil, despite outside circumstances. And that, my beautiful friends, is where some pretty incredible magic happens.

Referral

Serendipitous moments, listening when life speaks to you.

re•fer•ral
rəˈfərəl/
noun

An act of referring someone or something for consultation, review, or further action.

*The electricity in the air is palpable.
Look up at the sky, feel the stars. They are part of you.
Breathe in the moonlight. It too is part of you; You are
made up of all the magnificence of galaxies.*

Belinda Julian

I'm sure by now you all might be thinking "OK Lady, where is all this magic you speak of?" And to that, I say, it is all around you! It constantly surrounds each and every one of us. I've spoken endlessly about how the universe speaks to us to let us know how life is not working for us. Now we will dive deeper into How it says, *good job* you're on the right track, and gives us little winks, or says YES, keep going, you are heading in the right direction! Life is always speaking to us, and it is up to us to slow down enough to hear, see, or feel the cues we are given. Sometimes they can be like a giant green flashing light urging us forward. Other times it's a dull, almost faint yellow glow letting us know to get still within and pay attention.

I told the story of my moment of stillness when the idea for this book came to me only about an hour after having undeniable confirmation of my path moving forward. But it didn't stop with the one incident. A few days later, while driving, I had a flash of insight and immediately had the whole outline of my book. The same book I had no idea how to write. I mean, I didn't even go to high school! How the hell did it make any sense for me write a book? But I just kept listening. About a week later, I went to work, and one of my dear clients and I were having a conversation about strange happenings. In particular, it was about how her son was a super old soul, and that she herself regularly had visions of things happening before they happened. I went on to tell her about all these spiritual downloads I had been receiving and all the confirmations I was getting, letting me know they were in fact valid. Then I told her specifically about the day I had the vision, and how later that day I got the confirming validation. As I started to tell her about the lady coming up with the publishing house that I had pictured, she simultaneously blurted out, "Oh yeah!" and proceeded to say the exact same publisher I had visualized. We both started giggling uncontrollably; me at the pure magic that was unfolding around me, and she at her intuitive abilities, the beautiful gifts which I think she was just beginning to scratch the surface of.

Such a great experience this was, and just the fire I needed under my ass to propel me into making moves to bring my vision to life. Stories like that are what I call the big flashing green lights, guiding you to a life of purpose. It's the call to step into our greatness, and into our gifts, gifts we don't even know we possess. That is where spirit jumps in, using people, places, or occurrences to communicate with us in the best way so we will receive the messages. Other times it might be more subtle, a little less, WOW! in your face. But nevertheless, there is always an active conversation for those willing to listen. Other ways that I personally invoke or initiate guidance, and which I highly recommend to anyone who is open:

Dreams:

One of the quickest ways to access thoughts at a subconscious level is during our dream state. A whole lot of magic happens while we slumber, from healing on a cellular level, receiving guidance and direction, revealing unhealed parts of our psyche, recognizing untapped potential, and so much more. I have been keeping a dream journal for years. I have received all of those gifts, including deep healing, processing and transmuting subconscious blocks, precise guidance for wherever I was at that particular time and space, even prophetic dreams for myself or others. As with all other new endeavors, just start and practice. Keep a notebook handy and write down as much as you can recall upon waking while it is still fresh in your mind, before it gets washed away by everyday thoughts. You can look up specific symbols, meanings, or themes online, or look for a dream dictionary to refer to. Once you review and reflect on your journal, you will be blown away by how accurate and relevant it is to what's going on in your life. I have even written things down mindlessly, only to discover later that what I had dreamt actually transpired. Once you are in the habit of writing down your dreams, you can also ask for guidance, or any healing you need to be revealed to you while you sleep. Just write down your request before you go to bed, consciously choosing to be in a lucid dream state of receptivity.

Totems:

I mentioned previously that my early upbringing gifted me with the ability to be in tune with all around me. I could pick up on many of the subtle cues others would overlook. One of those ways is being in tune with the stirrings of the magical world we live in and the way it speaks to us if only we are willing to listen. This sometimes shows up as totems, both insects, and animals. Not just, *oh I saw a bird*, the same one I see all the time all around me that is very dominant in my area, but the ones that stand out and are a little rarer. I could probably write a whole chapter or more just on the random and divinely connected totems that have crossed my path and their very relevant and inspiring messages that accompanied them. Here are just a couple small examples. The first one was when I would be lagging on my writing even though I felt compelled to do it. I would be wrestling self-doubt, running on the hamster wheel in my brain rather than being productive. Randomly this woodpecker, had never before, appeared on this tree in my front yard, pecking away extremely hard to ignore. Basically, the short version of his message was, to make a plan and follow through with it.

Another time, while I was contemplating two different choices, a praying mantis appeared right next to the chair I always sit in on my porch. One of the many messages that accompanied this totem is to wait until the opportune time to make your move. Practice mindfulness as to your surroundings, and don't act out of haste instead of waiting until you're one-hundred percent certain it is time for movement.

Synchronicity:

This can happen in so many ways. You may have an inspired thought and then receive confirmation from people, a billboard, a song, etc. For example, regarding this book; my initial inspired idea, which was confirmed in multiple ways. Or maybe you are pondering a big change, going to an event, signing a paper, making some sort of decision; and one or more people bring up that very topic. If you are paying attention, you will know it is safe to move forward. Just say, thank you for the guidance and remember this prompt, this spiritual wink, was delivered just for you. The more you stay tapped in and aware, the more you will notice synchronicity occurring in your life. You will be able to feel that the magic is alive and at work in every moment. All of your life You will be reminded of the beautiful connectedness of all things, and that everything works in unison, even when we can't see it with our eyes. And the best part of all is there are no mistakes. Every single thing that occurs is for the growth of your soul and will reveal itself with the perfect timing.

Angels and Spirit Guides:

Another way to receive guidance, if you are open and receptive enough to bridge the veil between the unseen, is angels and spirit guides. We all have both surrounding us and able and willing to guide and direct us, if we only ask. Some common ways they let us know of their presence is coins, feathers, and number sequences. Some of the most common or highly recognized being 1111, 333, 555, 456, 123, along with those lines. I remember a few years back, I started seeing glimmers of light, sometimes above or around others. These days I also feel it when I look at people, generally, as soon as I'm still and not running a million miles an hour. There are specific meanings number sequences and combinations. Doreen Virtue has written whole books on the subject, but in general, number patterns are signposts letting you know everything is on track and going in the divine order of your higher purpose. I have experienced all of these on a regular basis. On a few occasions, I have even been sitting on my porch talking about something significant and literally had a feather drop down out of thin air. It feels so affirming, and pretty magical, I must say.

To some, all this may sound *whoo-hoo spiritual*, although I hope if this book has made its way to you, it is because its content will resonate with you. That doesn't have to be in its entirety. Instead, take whatever feels right to you, and discard all that doesn't. It's sort of like a *referral*. Keep the ones that serve you, and let the rest fall away. The next time you have a sign from the spirit world, know that it is sent just for you, to integrate into the alchemy that is you.

Extensions

Surrounding yourself with like-minded people.

ex•ten•sion
ˌik'sten(t)SH(ə)n/
noun

A part that is added to something to enlarge or prolong it; a continuation.

Surround
Yourself
with
beautiful
Loving
Souls.

Belinda Julian

Speaking of integrating; at this stage of the game, it is of utmost importance to be conscious of who and what we allow into our lives. Is it serving our growth into our highest selves? We may have grown accustomed to circumstances that contribute to us playing small, dumbing ourselves down, or silencing our truths. At some point, this will no longer work. I know for me, personally, I spent the majority of my life surrounded by people I was trying to make into better people. But they didn't really support my authentic growth other than showing me lessons I needed to learn about my value and worth. Once the lessons were acquired it was time to put them into action.

By this I mean surrounding yourself people who support your growth and expansion and vice versa. The time for one-sided relationships has come and gone, and with it the relationships with those who choose to complain, gossip, or operate at a low vibrational level. The alternative is choosing to be with the believers, the achievers, humanitarians, and people who want to improve our world in whatever way they can. They say you are the sum of the five people you surround yourself with the most. What does that look like in your life? It is not just about material success. Maybe one of your five has the innocence and naivety of a child, reminding you to let loose and have fun and not take things so seriously; that can be just as valuable as the friend who you have deep, stimulating, inspiring and uplifting conversations with. Each person has a specific role in your life; and a reflection of where you are, and what you are allowing and summoning into your life. My advice is to make sure your relationships are serving your fullest potential and highest aspirations.

Also become aware of the energy you are putting out. Are you leaving others better than before they met you? Are you adding value to their lives? Do they feel more uplifted or inspired after spending time in your presence? How are your daily interactions? This needn't be some huge shift. It can be as simple as how you interact with your grocery clerk or bank teller. Brighten someone's day by being loving and kind.

It's interesting that the more you find yourself coming from a loving, accepting place, you'll feel it sprinkled throughout all of your interactions. When we decide to show up from a place of love and acceptance in all our glory, we by default will show and inspire others to do the same whether we realize it or not. With so much going wrong or wacky in our world, it can be easy to become disheartened and discouraged. But know this, especially if you're one of the healers, helpers, and nurturers of the world, it all starts with you and me. Most of us would like to see changes in the world and are trying relentlessly to be everything to everyone. As cliché as it sounds, the change really starts with-in you; your internal space.

If each person were to be a master of their space and I believe this is starting to happen globally, that's when we will start seeing real, long-lasting changes. Each individual who is willing to take the time and commit to the sometimes-harrowing process of ripping the proverbial scab off of their wounds, doing the relentless work of cleaning them out no matter how painful, so that they may embody love is part of the solution. They no longer operate from their places of hurt, anger, frustration and old programming. Each person that makes the conscious choice to step into who they truly are rather than who their parents, society, and peers expect them to be, or have told them to be, are part of a real revolution. This my friends, is the foundation of the real change we wish to see in the world. It's about fighting for, and unraveling your true essence in a world that would probably prefer for you to stay *asleep*; asleep to the perfection that each of us is; asleep to the connectedness we all share.

There is still so much confusion and resistance as many choose to stay asleep and remain in the old way of doing things. But take a look around. Although there is much pain and sorrow in the world, there is a major uprising of love and connection, more acceptance of who we are without all of those societal labels. Social media, for example, can be viewed as an environment where we are less connected. But at the same time there are so many using their platform to raise awareness for a multitude of good; Body positivity, loving ourselves for who we are along with our "imperfections." Spiritual bad asses raising the collective consciousness. Self-love pioneers showing how to love and accept all the parts about ourselves we were told we shouldn't like. There is so much awareness and love rising; so many sharing their personal struggles and how they are overcoming them. Letting others know they aren't alone. Even though experiences may differ, we are all trying our best to understand ourselves, learning to have greater compassion for others, and offering grace to those who may have felt they would never receive it. And We're sharing the knowledge and wisdom we have acquired during our life thus far.

These are some of the things I see happening. I am hopeful this is the new trajectory. Not only is it essential to be mindful of our internal space, we also want to be aware of the energy we are putting out in the world; how we are treating others, and most importantly, how we are treating ourselves because this is what radiates out in the world. When we do this, we no longer seek to control or manipulate others and how they operate, nor do we need to. When we become a true example of living in love and truth, we become a model to which others naturally gravitate. They will be in awe, and wonder how we are able to hold a place of such peace and serenity no matter what is occurring around us. This is what I believe it truly means to be the change we wish to see in the world. My only bit of advice is this. Guard your space and shield yourself, at all cost, from those who feed off of your energy.

Discount

Not giving ourselves enough credit; selling yourself short.

dis•count
'diskount/
noun

noun: discount; plural noun: discounts
A deduction from the usual cost of something.

The compromises we make,
Convincing ourselves a pond will suffice when we crave
the ocean.
Wishing on a star, when we desire the entire universe;
Or that a little grey is okay when we desire clear blue
skies.

Belinda Julian

Guarding our energy means respecting and holding sacred our internal space; keeping it clear and free of fear and negativity that doesn't belong to us. Most importantly, it means doing that for ourselves every day. There may have been times in your life when you dulled your shine or quieted your voice for the comfort of others. Just as it is not our job to change others, or force our will upon them, it is no longer our task to placate others at our own expense. We no longer have to discount ourselves to make others comfortable. We can become so accustomed to thinking, behaving and feeling small, that it becomes habitual. While you may have had the seed planted that greatness is your birthright. There may still be times, purely from habit, you might find yourself in limbo between heart and ego and have moments of self-sabotage. This sabotage can look like a myriad of things; self-pity, berating yourself, feeling and believing you aren't as far along as you *should* or *could* be. You know how it goes. This is a prime example when it is oh so important to stop! breathe! reassess!

Take a moment to take inventory; even better if you can journal it, to refer back to at a later date. Take stock of everything that you have made it through thus far. Every single challenge that you not only survived but managed to thrive from. Reflect on every single thing has contributed to you being the beautiful masterpiece you are today, rich with all the wisdom your trials have gifted you. You are resilient in the way your heart has been able to expand and retract only to ultimately allow your soul the capacity to hold even more love and joy than you could have ever thought possible. Even in the times you couldn't possibly understand how things would get better or comprehend how events could be leading you in the right direction, to later realize it couldn't have worked out any better to move you forward, whether physically, emotionally, or spiritually to the exact place you needed to be. So, do yourself a favor and be gentle yourself, you are doing the best that you can. Especially in the moments when you feel like berating yourself for where you *aren't* yet, know, you are always precisely in the perfect place along your journey. Learning to lean into the valleys, so you can better appreciate the growth they bring, and making the peaks all the more worth it.

Know with every fiber of your being, that every circumstance is priming and prepping you, allowing you to grow into your most authentic self. With this, you may often find yourself in a void. When you are developing and evolving past all the pre-conceived notions of what family, friends, and society have told you should be, desire, and aspire to; When you have been following a script all your life that doesn't quite resonate with you any longer, you will inevitably feel that you're in a void. This void is necessary to give you time to re-evaluate, re-assess, and rebuild on a new foundation. The old structures will fall away, gifting you the opportunity to build on a more stable footing. This rebuilding is, in actuality, a beautiful thing. It is the epitome of the phoenix rising from the ashes.

Although at times it may feel nothing like the Phoenix; this void can be scary when things that used to bring you joy and happiness no longer seem to do so. You may realize that goals or dreams that you thought would bring peace and contentment, were never really yours. Believe me when I say, if you sit in this void without judging or shaming yourself, you will find that real lasting happiness and inner peace is on the other side of the not knowing. You will begin to seek within. You will learn to listen to that small, still voice that has been waiting to guide you in the direction of your most true bliss. You will learn to trust your inner being. You will learn that sometimes doing nothing is what you need to quiet the untruths you have been taught throughout your life. You will learn to use your inner compass rather than to question, berate or shame it.

You will naturally and effortlessly gravitate towards things, people, and situations that resonate with you on a soul level. You will no longer offer yourself to the world as half-truths, with a quivering faltering voice unsure of the magic that lives within you. You will no longer be scared of the power you possess deep within. When you stand in your truth and allow your purest essence to shine forth, the days of discounting yourself will be a thing of the past. With these new pillars, the pillars you have so bravely built will be a foundation, unlike anything you have ever known. You will have a faith rooted in knowledge. Knowing all that comes to be is for your highest good. You will no longer judge things as *good* or *bad* you will just know it is all necessary. You will trust you are always exactly where you are meant to be, and there are no mistakes.

Process

Faith in divine timing.

proc•ess
ˈprä͟ses,ˈprō͟ses/
noun.

A series of actions or steps taken to achieve a particular end.

With the change of seasons comes the time to rest our weathered hearts. Like the resetting of the clocks. Hit refresh and renew. We will shed the leaves that once served a purpose, leaving us bare and vulnerable; open to the season of change.

Belinda Julian

Knowing there are no mistakes in life helps ease the trepidation of the unknown and trust the process of your evolution. I think these days with the rising consciousness and growing numbers of people awakening to the fact that we create our realities, that we are the pioneers of our lives. We embrace the concept that our thoughts create our reality, and that what we feel internally is reflected in our lives in all ways and at all times. Along with this can be the *positivity* trap. While the goal is to shed all that is standing in our way of experiencing joy, happiness, and abundance, it is exactly that, a shedding process. This unveiling you are going through isn't always pretty, and most certainly is not comfortable.

If we fall into the new age trap that we are supposed to be only light and positivity, that can leave us in a battle with our humanness. It is true we are beings of light, and that is who we are at our core. But with that, we are just as much humans who are prone to human conditioning and at times human suffering. While we are striving to bring forth our spirit and operate from our soul, we mustn't fall prey to the ego mind which would like to make us feel bad when we aren't in this constant state of bliss. It is a delicate dance of nurturing the light while confronting the dark within, because it is in our darkest moments we begin to search for light; this IS the process.

On an individual basis and collectively, we are releasing and clearing lifetimes of shame, guilt, and pain of all sorts of magnitudes. We are successfully learning to live more conscious lives, even if at times it feels painstakingly slow. So, forgive yourself for not always being hyper-positive. Be kind as you balance the art of searching the dark recesses of old wounds you have stored, and shedding light on them with love, forgiveness, and understanding. I think the seed that has been planted is the acknowledgment of what has always been within. It just took something outside of you to trigger the inner knowing and wake you up.

We have been guided that if we master our thoughts, we will receive the grand reward of abundance, love and pretty much all we desire. Which we will, but it is not always a straight line to get there. It can be maddening at times as we race to this invisible finish line, falling in the comparison trap and forgetting to give ourselves the grace of being in this moment. We can become so outwardly focused that we miss that the point is to BE, FEEL, and ACCEPT the very moment we are in. When we can show up and be present, not weighed down by the depression of the past, or the anxiety of the future, this is indeed when one will experience all that we are seeking. Everything else is just stuff, and the icing on the proverbial cake.

What this means is learning to observe and acknowledge everything that comes to the surface. Observe it without attachment and judgment. Knowing even the bad is guiding you ever so consistently towards a life of joy. Our only job is to spend as much time doing that which brings us joy. This becomes easier and more habitual once we have gone through the process of observing and discarding all that does not bring joy. This process may sound relatively easy, and it is, but on different levels we can become addicted to our pain and attached to our suffering. On some dysfunctional level, we can even be tied to the highs and the lows of uncertainty for that feels normal to us.

So, this process of sorting through all that doesn't bring us joy and happiness, can be a confusing and uncertain time.

As you sift through and try out many different things you think will bring the inner peace you desire, only to realize it doesn't, or perhaps it does, but it is short-lived, you will be closer and closer to understanding it isn't the goal, the guy/girl, home, or job; but really what we are all seeking is the human connection, inner peace, purpose, and love. The simple reality is we already possess all of this and more, and the more time we spend integrating and embodying our inner light and spend time doing things that bring us joy, we then can share that with those around us, which is the next part of the *process*.

Gift certificate

Giving back

gift
gift/
noun

A thing given willingly to someone without payment; a present.

Even in our darkest hour know we can still be light to someone in need, and sometimes in giving we also inadvertently receive.

Belinda Julian

I can remember one particular day, the same day I wrote the quote you just read, I was having a terrible day, although of course now I cannot even begin to remember why. I recall having a beautiful conversation with a dear client of mine. Later on, when I got home and settled in, I received a message from her letting me know that just me being there and being present with her and listening, brightened her day and helped her out of the funk she had been in. Where am I going with this, you may ask? Giving back doesn't always have to be in some magnificent way. It can be as simple as really being present when someone needs a listening ear. It can be gazing compassionately into someone's eyes and holding gaze to let them know they aren't alone, that someone values them and truly sees them. The possibilities to share and spread joy to others is endless and doesn't require you to be at some self-imposed image of strength, happiness, abundance or financial requirement means.

Giving back can be a donation or service based, but can just as well be a simple compliment meant to brighten someone's day. What you will find with any act of kindness is it honestly works double time in making you feel good as well. As a matter of fact, when we feel the most profound complacency, depression, or anxiety we are much too focused on ourselves and just the act of focusing on serving others will instantly and consistently make us feel better. It draws our focus outward, rather than staying fixated internally.

When you are ready to take this a step further, when you have slain your most daunting dragons and are feeling and operating from a full cup, you aren't seeking validation or wishing to gain something from giving; this is the sweet spot, and usually when quite naturally you will feel a call to share your passions, whatever they may be, with the world. This doesn't need to be in some monumental way, but what it can and will be is anything you feel curious about, or have a natural affinity toward. Something that brings you joy, and by default will bring joy to others. This pleasure can and will be many things, but it will most likely involve some form of creation.

We are all meant to create! Many people stop or never start creating because their stories got in the way. I'm not perfect at doing such and such. I don't know how. I'm not creative, and so on. But I am here to remind you, we are all creators. Sure, we may not be the next Picasso, or Beyoncé, but we all have our natural gifts, which belong to, and are specific to only us. Our purpose is just to create, without limitation, without letting our wounds, our past, our EGO, run the show. When you can do this; create without restriction what you believe you are capable of, without judgment of your make-believe shortcomings, and without expectation of how things will turn out, or how it will be received, this is where the real magic will happen.

You need not have everything figured out, or know what the outcomes will be, but I do believe we are meant to share our gifts with others. Again, it does not have to be some particular skill set. Just your full presence alone, is a gift to others when you show up in your wholeness. Read this next sentence three times and let it soak in! You are a gift, just the way you are. Yes, just the way you are now, in all the messiness, all the uncertainty, all of your past, and mainly because of your history.

You are valuable! Even if at times you don't feel it or recognize it.

You are worthy! Even if no one ever taught you this truth, and you have stumbled through life trying to believe this to be true.

My advice is to move forward regardless of your past. Create just because it makes you feel good. Paint, dance, write, sing. Try new things, suck at them, be mediocre at it, practice till you get better, fail at things. It's all ok, better than ok, it is fantastic! You are becoming who you have not yet been. Which means trying all sorts of things that are new. Most importantly, break out of self-imposed limitations and ego driven mental blocks. It's all part of the evolution of you. And when you do find thing or *things* that let you be who you are, your highest self, share them with friends, family, in your community, online, and offline. Whatever your particular talents may be; your wisdom, your experience, your creation, it's yours to share.

I'll leave you with a little story about My grandmother, who unfortunately met an untimely death after being hit by a careless driver while riding her motorized scooter. While my family and I gathered to celebrate her life, and reflect on her legacy, I realized that at times I had felt pity for my grandmother because she had led a life void of many luxuries. She lived in a tiny trailer in a mobile home park in the middle of nowhere. As I began writing about my grandmother and the impact her life had on all of us, it dawned on me that her life had been pretty incredible. She was a living breathing example of how more of us should aspire to live. Above all else, she was kind, to anyone and everyone she met. She always had the curiosity of a young child learning as much as she could whether it was a new class, or a new book she was soaking up. She marveled at the beauty of the world we lived in and spent much of her time outdoors in the simple yet astounding beauty that is available to us all. Best of all, she was always creating. From the hand embroidered cards, she made and sent to everyone on their birthdays, to intricate jewelry she created and sold at local markets, or gifted to friends and family, to cooking and baking, and winning local fair competitions, her life added beauty to the world. Her legacy is one I think anyone could look at and see her life was full of textures and experience. She truly lived, as we all should, with curiosity and kindness in our hearts. A mind that is full of ideas just waiting to be fulfilled in the act of creation. The mindfulness to enjoy the abundance of nature that surrounds us. And last, but not least, the gift of community, both in the gifts she bestowed on others, and connections she shared. I no longer think she lived a small life but instead modeled in its entirety a life lived to its fullest.

Solution

You are the solution you seek.

so•lu•tion
sə'lo͞oSH(ə)n/
noun

A means of solving a problem or dealing with a difficult situation.

We must learn to break out of the chrysalises of our minds.

Belinda Julian

The solution. What does that mean? Being a hairdresser the solution is what you mix with the color or bleach to activate it; I hope if you gain one thing from these writings, it's that it initiates a recognition of the perfection that already exists within you. Because whether it's this book, another book, a seminar, or any other source, none of it is anything you don't already have within. Sometimes it just takes another voice to awaken and remind you of what you already know. And that is that YOU ARE the solution just waiting to be activated. You are whole and complete already, and you always have been.

Take for example the concept of us as babies, being perfect, receiving all that we need just by existing. But as we grow we are silenced; taught to play small, bombarded by others who have forgotten their perfection and who project their fears and thoughts of being incomplete on us. And then we take those thoughts on as our own and begin to search for things outside of us to bring what we think will make us whole. For so many of us, it takes years if ever to silence the outside world so that they do not continue to make up our inner world; so that we may hear the ever-present truth, THE UNIVERSAL TRUTH.

YOU ARE PERFECT.
YOU DON'T NEED TO SEEK LOVE. YOU ARE LOVE.
YOU HAVE EVERYTHING WITHIN.

When you can let this one truth, your perfection, permeate your being, letting go of the inner conflict you carry, you create space to be free. Free to receive everything life is waiting to give you once you release the barriers that keep you from being receptive. On the subject of inner conflict, the only reason it is conflict is that deep within, your soul knows your truth but your ego made up of your wounds, fears, perceived inadequacies, and your stories tries to convince you of a make-believe truth. Contemplate that for a moment. When you have those moments of inner battle, know that the only reason you are feeling conflicted is that you are going against your truth. It is your soul crying out to stop being at war with yourself.

Imagine for a moment how freeing it is to just be, without judging yourself for your human emotions when they come up, but instead just observing them and feeling them as they are meant to be explored, and then moving on. By cutting out the middle man, your ego-self, you free up so much time that can be better used to love, create, and live in peace.

In truth, so many of the times I felt things were genuinely horrific in my life, it was usually only in my head. I either made up scenarios of impending doom in the near or far future, or was tormented by recreations of past experiences. There were even times when something or someone got a rise out of me, and I created a story around it or them. Little did I know I always had the choice to be at peace, in all circumstances and at all times.

Think of the areas of your life where you are still in resistance with yourself and how you can soften within, just by being. Think of how you can be gentler with yourself. How you can find this sweet spot of just being without fear of the future or feeling shame from the past. Without taking things personally and without making the problems of others as your own. When you can be in this space of calm receptivity and tolerance, your real power will be in the forefront at all times and in all ways. You will then realize that you are, and have always been, the SOLUTION! You hold power to end needless suffering from your existence. It is not all the things outside of you that you have grown accustomed to seeking to fill the inner void. Now you will know they were all temporary.

Return to the pure perfection of your youth; of your inner child, the one inside of you that loves unconditionally, and wholeheartedly.

The little you that plays and creates just because it is joyful.

The inner you that lets your needs and wants to be known, unashamed at the request, and never entertaining the notion that your requirements will not be fulfilled.

The soul that guides you will always lead you to the right decisions, perfectly crafted for your personal growth.

Follow this you! Own the fact that you are the solution! Tuning in to all that activates this great awareness in you, knowing that you don't need to fix or change anything. You've only ever needed to turn the lights on in your own home. To illuminate the brilliance that has always been inside.

Dedication

I would like to dedicate this book to all my beautiful friends and family who believed in me and listened to me carry on relentlessly during all the stages of writing this book; who saw this creation from its incubation stage to full fruition, celebrating and encouraging me at every single milestone. In particular, my son Vincent who has and will always be my driving force, my inspiration to do and be the best that I can, always reminding me to listen to my inner stirrings, and trust the process of life.

About the author

Belinda Julian, with all her years behind the chair as a Hairstylist combined with her passion for self-improvement, has a natural ability for understanding the human connection and human condition. Her gift of empathy and communication is something she believes is inherent and meant to be shared. Aside from dressing hair and sharing love through writing. You will find her most days enjoying the company of friends and family or having her next adventure with her beloved son.

Printed in the United States
By Bookmasters